A chance to change

A chance to change

Access, citizenship and sustainability in open learning

Paul Fordham
John Fox
Patrick Muzaale

NIACE
THE NATIONAL ORGANISATION FOR ADULT LEARNING

intermedia

Published by the National Institute of Adult Continuing Education (England and Wales)
21 De Montfort Street, Leicester, LE1 7GE
Company registration no. 2603322
Charity registration no. 1002775
The NIACE website on the Internet is http://www.niace.org.uk

First published 1998

In association with Intermedia PO Box 39483, Nairobi, Kenya
Intermedia provides consultancy in community development, training design, human resource development and project support communication for the education, health, housing and agricultural sectors. Intermedia has undertaken work in Latin America and Asia as well as Africa.

CATALOGUING IN PUBLICATION DATA
A CIP record for this title is available from the British Library
ISBN 1 86201 043 9

Typeset by The Midlands Book Typesetting Co., Loughborough
Text design by Virman Man
Cover design by Boldface
Printed in Great Britain by The Loose Leaf Company

Contents

Acknowledgements

This book could not have written without the enthusiastic support of former students and staff of the College of Social Studies. In particular we have to thank all those who took the trouble to come to the seminars arranged in Kenya and Uganda, as well as those who gave freely of their time to fill in bio data forms and to respond to interviews. The Nairobi seminar, chaired by former governor Hon. J.J Nyagah, was the essential starting point for tracing other respondents. The authors were also helped by Joe Mwaniki in tracing the present whereabouts of other former students, and by Tom Mulusa, who conducted the interviews in western Kenya.

Colleagues who had been members of the teaching staff also gave freely of their time in responding to our requests for interviews, sometimes in person (either in east Africa or the UK) and sometimes by long distance telephone. They include: Sheila Gifford (formerly Fordham), Brian Harvey, June Knowles, Roger Leys, Picton Mbatha, Tom Mulusa, Godfrey Muriuki, John Nottingham, Peter Temu, Helen Wamere, Mark Wheeler and Sally Wheeler.

The case study was conducted during 1995–96 with the help of generous grants from the Dulverton and Leverhulme Trusts. The writing is the result of close co-operation between the former Principal of the CSS (Paul Fordham), a former tutor (John Fox, now head of Intermedia Ltd, Nairobi) and a former student (Patrick Muzaale, at that time Professor of Social Work and Social Administration at Makerere University). Comments by Lalage Bown, Ada Fordham and Veronica McGivney on earlier drafts, were very helpful indeed in helping us to complete and improve on what we had written.

Preface

The case study around which this book is written stresses two of the enduring themes of liberal adult education: access to higher education for mature students and education for citizenship. Both these themes were echoed in the work of the 1997 UNESCO conference in Hamburg on *Adult Learning: a key for the twenty-first century.* The promotion of 'active citizenship', democracy and human rights within cultural diversity, and access to post-secondary education through open learning systems were both important Conference themes. Thus the themes themselves are part not only of the liberal tradition in Britain, but also of continuing adult education discourses in the context of increasing globalisation of the world economy. We return to these themes in the final chapter, which looks at how this kind of adult learning might be promoted and sustained into the next century; and in what contexts.

This book has its origins in a study of the career paths of students from one particular residential college for adult education. The college was established by adult educators from Britain and, in the UK terminology of the time (the 1960s), it was seen as a mixture of a 'short term' and a 'long term' college. In the case of the UK, the latter have been more enduring than the former. While many of the short term colleges have been closed, only one of the much smaller number of long term colleges suffered the same fate under the harsh financial and unfriendly political regime of the1980s; and one new one was opened (Northern College). Similarly, in our case study, it was the 'long' course programme which had the greatest impact.

In pursuing our study of the short life of the College of Social Studies (CSS) at Kikuyu in Kenya (1961 to 1970), we began to ask ourselves not only about the particular successes and failures of this one college, but also more generally about the social and political circumstances in which adult learning programmes, in any context, can be sustained. In doing so, we developed a framework for analysis which focuses on context and sustainability; we believe this has general applicability and can be used to analyse adult learning programmes in any context. The framework ('Conditions for sustaining adult learning programmes') is outlined in Chapter 1.

The two main themes of the book follow from the original mission at Kikuyu and from the personal career motivation of the long-course students.* The latter were concerned above all with access to higher education for those without formal entry qualifications. The College itself accepted the validity of this motivation, but also tried to maintain its original mission of civic education for active participation in the public life of a young democracy.

When former students came to a Reunion and Seminar in Nairobi in March 1995, they were clear about the considerable impact on their lives of the College's one year course. In the words of Silas Ita, the impact was 'double edged'. First, it offered the opportunity of individual advancement for mature students whose previous educational opportunities had been limited; second, it enabled 'better judgement and decision making in day to day life and management issues and national development issues.'[1]

At one level this book must therefore be about a cultural transplant – the outcome of which was certainly unpredictable at the time. From the evidence of the ex-students, it seems to have been successful both in tapping hidden talent and also in training for leadership, decision making and responsibility. But as an institution it was too short lived to make a lasting social impact. What impact there was came from the abilities, energy and vision of those who had benefited from the programme. A significant proportion of former students became influential in their various occupations and organisations. Thus it is only through the lives and ideas of individuals, and from a comparative analysis of the background ideas and action, that useful judgements can be made about future possibilities.

Kampala, Nairobi and Shrewsbury 1996–97

Note

[1]Fordham, Fox and Muzaale 1995

*In the ten years from 1961, more than 100 mature students attended the short course programme and about 130 its long course (one academic year, initially, squeezed into seven months)

Chapter 1

Adults learning: purposes and sustainability

A framework for analysis

In deriving the framework for analysis, we have drawn both on the case study and on comparative experience from other countries and cultures. The comparative examples included in the section below are all based on real situations within the professional experience of the authors. It is suggested that they may be useful both in programme planning and in the review of existing programmes during regular programme monitoring.

Changes in any one of the ten conditions for sustainability may require a rapid response from the directors, organisers and teachers of adult learning programmes. And yet staff can be both confused and bewildered when the external context changes and they have not thought through how best to respond. One example from the UK is the rapid demise of non-credit courses in British universities once the external funding arrangements were withdrawn. Another is the decline in importance of the Institute of Adult Education in Dar es Salaam once basic adult literacy had reached more than 80 per cent of the population and adult learning needs began to change faster than the Institute set up to provide for them. The importance of a rapid response to changed external circumstances is one reason why we suggest the framework may have usefulness beyond this particular study.

Conditions for sustaining adult learning programmes

1. The programme addresses a real need (as perceived by the programme designers, external agencies, or potential participants).

This relates to how educational activities are identified; the providing agency might, for example, be seizing an opportunity (in a marketing sense) or responding to demands by intending participants.

In the UK, an entrepreneurial television broadcaster did quite a lot of research into the most popular courses being provided in further education centres, and he then invested a considerable sum of money in producing a range of educational video tapes – on such topics as car maintenance, gardening and cookery. The project failed because not enough people bought the tapes; either because they preferred to attend 'traditional' classes – or they made pirate copies.

2. It harmonises with the mission of the providing agency.

The second question the directors and staff will (or should) ask is whether the identified programme fits in with the agreed purpose, objectives and values of the agency.

In Kenya, in 1968, the staff of the University of Nairobi Institute of Studies decided not to accede to the Government's request that it should promote extra-mural classes based on the ruling party's economic and social policy statement, the Sessional Paper No.10 – because it believed that it would not be allowed to treat key issues in an impartial and critical manner.

In Tanzania, in the mid-eighties, the Institute of Adult Education came under criticism (from both within and without) for putting most of its resources into providing fee-paying secondary school courses for teenagers.

3. It is permitted or tolerated by the controlling authorities (the state, or other concerned authority).

If a programme is seen to be such that it takes up an undue amount of revenue, or it might lead to conflict among people, or offend the agreed norms of decency within the society – or threaten in any way the position of a ruling group, then the programme might not be allowed by any institution or government that has any kind of controlling authority over the providing agency.

In India, in the mid 1980s, the then national literacy programme was much reduced in size (it was widely assumed) because it was not only an extremely expensive operation, but also because it was raising people's awareness of social injustices – and arousing expectations that could not be met without a massive shift in resource allocations.

4. It secures sufficient financial support.

Money to run the programme has to be secured either through state subsidy, or from interested non-governmental organisations, or from fees paid by the participants themselves.

Non-credit liberal studies in British universities and leisure-related courses in local authority further education centres were severely curtailed in the early nineties when the Department for Education grants for such activities were drastically cut.

5. It is organised, promoted and taught by staff with a clear understanding and acceptance of the providing agency's mission – and with the required professional competence.

This condition relates to whether the programme is able to recruit and deploy organisers, teachers or trainers with both a sense of what the providing agency is set up to achieve, and with sufficient knowledge and skill to promote its activities in an effective manner, teach the participants what they are supposed to learn – and induct staff so that they are left in no doubt as to the mission of the agency or the demands of particular educational programmes.

In a British Extra-Mural Department, an Industrial Relations tutor resigned when he was restrained by the Head of Department from teaching health service workers how to occupy hospitals when engaged in strike action.

In an American University Department of Continuing Education a group of educators engaged in a Masters in Adult Education course protested to the directors that they were wasting their time on a particular unit, because the teacher knew less about his subject – the psychology of adult learning – than they did.

6. It attracts participants in sufficient numbers.

If no-one (or too few) people wish to follow a particular course, then it will fail to get off the ground.

In a Workers' Educational Association programme in Britain, when the question of whether Britain should join the European Common Market was being fiercely debated in the newspapers and on television, a well-advertised course on the matter attracted only one student – whereas all four Introduction to Geology courses were oversubscribed.

7. Its curriculum is seen as relevant to the needs and interests of the various stakeholders (participants, providing agency, sponsors, etc.)

A course may be seen to be desirable (or even necessary) by the providing agency and the controlling authorities – but its contents and the methods do not suit the agreed objectives.

In northern Ghana, men and women farmers who were being sent by their Chiefs to a nine-month residential centre run on the lines of a Scandinavian folk high school were resentful because not only were their farms suffering from their absence, but also because a course which was supposed to be teaching them farming and other income-generating skills was focusing on non-commercial crafts such as weaving and music-making.

8. It deploys an adequate range of learning materials.

It is not easy to learn how to fly an aircraft without an aircraft to fly – or at least a simulator to practise on.

In the early eighties in the Institute of Adult Education in Dar es Salaam a 60-hour unit on the use of audio visual aids was being given to the students on the Diploma in Adult Education course – although the Institute did not even possess working models of some of the aids that featured on the course, such as video cameras and overhead projectors. In the University of Dar es Salaam, during the same period, undergraduate and graduate degree courses in Adult Education were being taught to large numbers of students – even *though the university library possessed only three texts that were of any relevance to the subject.*

9. The teaching is carefully matched to the educational background and capacities of the participants.

If a course is pitched at too high (or remote) a level, then it either fails to communicate – or it simply fails.

'He is obviously a very clever man,' said a mineworker of the Oxford Lecturer in Economics who had just been teaching for an hour and a half, 'because I didn't understand anything of what he was saying.'

A module of a WHO management training programme on the incidence and prevalence of TB – which demanded a grasp of fairly sophisticated techniques for statistical analysis – was presented without modification to a group of clinical officers who were having difficulty in working out simple percentages.

10. The learning environment is appropriate for both learners and curricula.

If the environment cannot be adapted to the teaching style or is not appropriate for the learners, then they will be less likely to attend or to learn effectively.

In the Egyptian adult literacy programme it was found that some female learners were unwilling to attend mixed classes or to do so in schoolrooms after children had gone home. When they moved to meeting places in the courtyards of private houses, they were also able to alter the timing of meetings to avoid times which clashed with their family responsibilities.

As well as giving the framework for analysis of the case study, the comparative experiences outlined above also provide a means for setting its main themes in a wider international context which is relevant for the 1990s and beyond.

It has been argued that of the four basic functions of adult education (administration, teaching, counselling and programme planning), only the last named has no clear analogue in initial education.

> *The uniqueness and centrality of the program development function in adult education derives ultimately from the diversity of purposes and needs adult educators and adult agencies must address. The curricula of schools and colleges tend to be relatively uniform and to remain fairly stable over time.*[1]

Now, as the examples illustrate, while adult educators have been skilled at deriving new and innovative programmes, once 'success' (often defined as a good attendance rate) has been achieved, there is a tendency to repeat the old formulae and to expect continued success, even when the context changes. If as much attention were given to monitoring (including the monitoring of changing contextual variables) as to the initial planning processes, then the conditions for securing sustainability would be foreseen more easily. The authors intend that the ten conditions outlined above should be used as a possible check list when monitoring any adult learning programmes, developed both for the multiplicity of purposes and in the many contexts in which adult educators work.

Introduction to the Kikuyu case study

The original aim of the College of Social Studies was to provide a place where East Africans (mainly from Kenya, but also from Uganda, Tanganyika and Zanzibar) could talk about economic, social and political development – in the jargon of the time, 'nation building'. Behind this broadly political aim lay an assumption that liberal democracies – which it was hoped would be created in east Africa – should be promoted in part by the liberal education of the adult population.

The first Principal asserted that the College could 'help Kenya in the twentieth century as adult education helped Britain in the nineteenth, to pass through a difficult period of social change . . . not to produce specialists, but citizens who are better informed about the issues of the day, better able to play their part in dealing with them'. And he went on to suggest this could be achieved by helping students 'get a firmer hold upon the basic techniques of study and the arts of communication'.[2]

The roots of the College lay in a long tradition of civic education in the UK; this stressed the importance of rational thought and analysis as essential components of democratic debate and government. It also emphasised both public service and individual self-fulfilment as part of the struggle for social justice and emancipation. In the case of the UK, this stress on social justice had focused on the inequalities arising from social class divisions (and much later those of gender), while in east Africa in the 1960s the stress was on ensuring African emancipation and advancement.

What lay at the heart of the 1960s experiment at Kikuyu was an educational programme derived from the UK liberal tradition, a tradition which stemmed from a particular idea of citizenship (explored in Chapter 8 on *Learning and training for active citizenship*). Part of this tradition was that adult learners should be educated as confident and active individuals *within society*; and in this tradition, access to university, or personal career development, were secondary purposes which might or might not be part of the mission of particular providing institutions. Nevertheless, as this case study shows, they were often important motivating factors for the adult learners themselves. And a 1962 study from Ruskin College in Oxford[3] shows much the same drive for additional academic qualifications and for upward career mobility.

Although the underlying social purpose at Kikuyu was not seen as important by all staff, and eventually became attenuated to the point of extinction, the curriculum and style of teaching, the whole academic culture of the College, was one derived from the Oxford tutorial system and from liberal adult education as then practised in the Nottingham University Department of Adult Education. There was certainly more *overt* emphasis on individual educational ambitions than would have been true in the UK; but even in the UK, nobody doubts that a good Oxford or Nottingham education – even if pursued in the first instance at an adult education college – is other than a passport to good employment opportunities. What this book suggests is that there was a clear link between the kind of 'good' education then on offer and the use that the students made of their opportunities for learning.

When former student Silas Ita described the Kikuyu experience as 'double edged', he was in fact bringing together part of the original mission of extending active citizenship and the overwhelming student motivation of personal advancement. In seeking to understand those aspects of the experience which made for the double-edged success at Kikuyu in the 1960s, the book explores what appear to be the generalisable and transferable components of the programme. Our main emphases are on the sustainability of adult learning for individual access to higher education, for socio-economic development and for the promotion of civic awareness/participation in particular contexts. In Chapter 8 we analyse the essential *educational* components of the liberal tradition and explore in the final chapter how these might be used in future programmes for adult learners.

Some aspects of the case study experiences can be explained by the special circumstance of Kenya in the 1960s. However, the more interesting questions are still live issues today. In the 'globalised' world of the late 1990s, is there a place for a college or for educational programmes which offer a training both for responsible citizenship and for individual growth and advancement? If there is, what form should these take and in what circumstances? These questions are explored in the final chapters of the book.

Notes

[1]Darkenwald and Merriam 1982 :16
[2]Wiltshire 1961
[3]Blumler 1962

Chapter 2

The case study: stakeholders and antecedents

The arguments we put forward are built around the experiences of those who came to the one-year course. This was designed to prepare able but unqualified adults for university entry. As an access programme, the one year ('long') course attracted those individuals who wanted to upgrade their qualifications and so find better jobs. Their aim was to pass a Certificate of Adult Studies (recognised for a time in Kenya as equivalent to 'A' level) and also the Mature Age Entrance examination of the University of East Africa.

The College as originally conceived lasted for only ten years. It was created as an independent College with its own Board of Governors, but it became a Department of the University College Nairobi in 1963. After 1969, the one-year course was abandoned and its residential programme became concentrated on adult education training for other educational providers. Nearly 20 years later, in 1988, and because of the pressure of undergraduate numbers in the University of Nairobi, the existing Diploma course in Adult Education was also abandoned and the former College of Social Studies (residential capacity 60 students) was absorbed into a newly-built 2,000+ undergraduate campus. The only activity for mature adults still existing in 1996 was the part-time degree programme offered mainly by correspondence.

However, although the University of Nairobi has absorbed what was left of the College, it was not one of the original stakeholders. In fact, it was as a free-standing institution that the College of Social Studies quickly established a reputation for integrity, and was seen by some as a focus of study independent of the colonial past. For example, in early 1963, one of the junior university lecturers in history approached the Principal about the possibility of employment because he was unhappy about working in the then University College, which he saw as dominated by expatriate staff. But the university connection was made later in the same year and, because it was thought inappropriate to have a college within a college, was renamed Adult Studies Centre in 1966.

What is significant for our purposes is that the University of Nairobi did not start the College, but it did succeed in closing it! It was not there in the beginning, and many of those who studied and worked there in the 1960s now think (with the wisdom of hindsight) that the connection was a mistake. This is an argument which is taken up in Chapter 9.

Stakeholders

So who were the original stakeholders, what was their importance at the time of the establishment and early operation of the College, and how did both they and the balance of power and influence between them change over time? Of the four main sets of stakeholders, neither the **students** nor most of the **tutors** were in place until 1961–62; the **wider polity** (including the Colonial Government and the various local political interest groups then competing for future power) was in flux until independence in December 1963. This gave the fourth group of stakeholders, the **founders** (including the first two Principals) unusually pivotal positions during the pre-history of the College (1958–61) and the early years of its operation to about 1965. But the founders were by no means a united group (and some were greatly influenced by the debates within the wider polity); however, it was the outcome of the power struggles within that group that determined the character of the College during the ten years of its operation.

The founders

Capricorn Africa Society

The College had its origins in ideas which were publicised at a Conference on Education for Nationhood held in Nairobi in 1958 and sponsored by the Capricorn Africa Society. Capricorn had a brief political importance both in Rhodesia and in Kenya, at a time when the white settler interests in those countries were trying to come to terms with growing African demands for socio-economic equality and for political independence. Capricorn saw the 'heady wine' of African nationalism as something which was undesirable in itself, and something that could be countered by reducing the social isolation of the various racial groups – albeit in carefully controlled circumstances:

> *Peoples with different colours, religions, cultures, from country and urban areas, and different social classes can, by a fuller understanding of their spiritual as well as material interdependence, achieve a sense of common national purpose, and live together as a community.*

This common national purpose was to be developed by all races under the tutelage of non-Africans. Capricorn existed:

> *to give Europeans and Asians a real understanding of the frustrations at present driving the Africans towards racial nationalism; and to give them a sense of responsibility for the removing of these frustrations and a knowledge of how they could help them to do so.*

The Capricorn Chairman envisaged the 'marriage of the Capricorn idea with the Folk High School educational techniques' which had earlier been so successful in national regeneration in Scandinavia. This 'could bring about the revolution in people's thinking which we all know to be vital to Africa's future.'[1]

The 1958 Conference carefully excluded the 'light-hearted drinkers of the heady wine of African nationalism' and, of the 29 patrons of the Conference, only eight were African. The main outcome was a resolution calling for the establishment of colleges of citizenship in Kenya and in Rhodesia (Ranche House College in Harare still flourishes). However, this was not simply a talking shop. The UK-based Dulverton Trust (which had strong links with Kenya business interests) had supported the Conference and was now prepared to finance the implementation of the resolution. An Association of the Kenya College of Citizenship was formed, with a Management Committee to oversee the details. It was this Committee which was eventually to evolve into the Board of Governors for the College.

In the event, the creation of the new structure was crucial. It brought about the domination of local business interests and, eventually, the exclusion of Capricorn's political ideas. It was perhaps unfair to castigate Capricorn's educational policies as no more than 'multi-racial tea parties'; but the first Principal was certainly right in thinking that by 1960 it was no longer possible to select students on the basis of racial origin and that Capricorn had by then become a spent political force.

The colonial government

At one level, the ideas of Capricorn were in tune with the ideas of citizenship and nationhood already put forward by the Colonial Office ten years earlier. The CO argued that education for citizenship should be carried out 'with comparatively small groups of leaders'. The aim was for the colonies to 'attain responsible self government', and for colonial peoples 'to tread the path of evolutionary democracy' under British tutelage.

However, the Colonial Office had seldom been wholly in tune with the thinking of white settler groups. Certainly by the late 1940s and 50s, and starting in West Africa, the whole trend was to work with the growing nationalist movements – to control what might have been seen as excesses, but certainly to lead towards democratic self government. It should be remembered that with the election of a Labour government in 1945, and especially with the appointment as Secretary of State for the Colonies a Minister with a known anti-colonial record – Arthur Creech-Jones – the whole impetus within the British Government changed away from preservation of the status quo towards those who had been working towards controlled change. The 1948 Report on *Education for Citizenship in Africa*, believed that education for citizenship should include the protection of minority interests, but that it should also find ways of using the 'abundant energy' of national movements 'in constructive work for the common benefit'[2].

By contrast, the citizenship envisaged by Capricorn was not merely paternalistic in the Colonial Office sense, but it sought a narrow multi-racialism under the continued leadership of the settler interests. Whereas the Colonial Office came to espouse non-racial solutions to the problems of self-government,

Capricorn sought an equal balance between blacks, whites and Asians – when the population balance was most unequal.

Colonial Office ideas about citizenship had earlier been included in its widely influential paper, *Mass Education in African Society* of 1944. This made explicit the link between education and political development, and called for an education which would inspire a constructive citizenship embracing the active participation of community leaders. To be effective, 'there must be provision in mass education to secure freedom of discussion and criticism, and there must be opportunity for extending the range of knowledge relevant to the changing conditions'[3]. However, for our analysis, it is the emphasis given to the political role of *adult* education, provided particularly but not exclusively through university outreach, which is most significant.

The Elliott and Asquith Reports of 1945, which made recommendations for new university institutions in British colonies, initiated an adult education role for the newly established African universities by recommending the establishment of extra-mural departments. By the time Capricorn convened the Nairobi conference, Makerere University College from Uganda had already been active extra-murally in Kenya for some two years. And it was always intended to make the connection with other kinds of adult education and with social movements, including the rise to political power of new social classes, the importance of voluntary associations, and the need for a 'firm grasp on the distinction between education and propaganda'. In particular, there was a growing appreciation of the relevance of the Danish Folk High School idea:

> *By the study of national history and culture, with some economic and political discussion and practical work in farming, they have trained successive generations of one of the most progressive rural and stable democratic countries in the world.*

While commending the experimental work of Oxford University's Extra-Mural Delegacy in West Africa, the 1948 Report on Education for Citizenship also called for 'steps to be taken to bring young and progressive Colonial people into contact with those who are working in this field in Europe'. It recommended that not only should representatives of democratic adult education movements go from Britain to work in the Colonies, but Colonial workers should go to Britain to share in British and European experience.[4] This contact with the wider adult education movement in Britain, was to be crucial to the development of the College of Social Studies.

British and local business interests

In the aftermath of the 1958 conference, the Dulverton Trust appointed consultants to work out detailed plans for the new College. At the same time it was becoming increasingly disillusioned with the capacity of Capricorn to deliver local support and enthusiasm. Lord Kilmaine, the Trust's Secretary, concluded that

Capricorn 'did not command sufficient confidence among the European industrial and commercial enterprises, which are the main source of finance'.

In order to move ahead as rapidly as possible,* Lord Dulverton visited Nairobi in April 1959 and staged a coup within the Management Committee. A new Board of Governors was appointed (including only one Capricornist, Mrs Susan Wood) and with the key figures of Sir Philip Rogers (later Chairman) and Sir Donald MacGillivray as the Trust's trustees in Kenya.

To start off the College, £35,000 was offered, but none of this could be spent without the approval of the two newly appointed trustees. Sir Philip (then Chairman of the East African Tobacco Company) and Sir Donald (then farming in Kenya but a recently retired colonial Governor) were to be the key figures in wresting control from Capricorn and in ensuring the support of local business interests.

The dispute with Capricorn rumbled on for some time in public, even after the College had appointed its first Principal. But by August the same year Lord Kilmaine was already threatening to withdraw the proffered funds and Capricorn effectively capitulated to local business interests. Its Chairman, Michael Wood, announced that he would circulate all members to say that in future no mention of Capricorn should be made in connection with the College. As Lord Kilmaine himself wrote in the following year, '. . . the Dulverton Trust snatched the College away from the organisation which had first conceived the idea of it, on the ground that the organisation was incompetent to translate the idea into action'.[5]

At the time of the Dulverton coup, the new Governors acquired their first African member, Musa Amalemba. And, in 1960, came the appointment of J J Nyagah, the second African governor, later a senior Minister in all post-independence Governments until his retirement in 1993. In 1995 it was he who gave the keynote address at the Student Reunion and Seminar. With the appointment of these two governors, the process of accommodation to the African majority had begun.

British adult educators

One of the chosen instruments for citizenship education identified by the Colonial Office was the UK 'adult education movement'. In the aftermath of war, from 1944 onwards, voluntary bodies such as the Workers' Educational Association and Women's Institutes, university adult education or extra-mural departments, and new residential colleges running a range of short courses – all these institutions and organisations flourished. Moreover, the success of staff directing the war-time Army Bureau of Current Affairs (ABCA), provided a pool of skilled people with new and varied experiences in the education of adults who were looking for similar opportunities in civilian life.

When the Dulverton Trust wanted to conduct a feasibility study into the

*Kilmaine argued that 'events in Africa are rushing forward with appalling rapidity, and if this multi-racial college is to be in time to make any contribution towards saving anything from the rising tide of nationalism, it should get into action at the earliest possible moment.

citizenship college idea they selected a two-person team of Mr and Mrs Hunter. Guy Hunter had ABCA experience, and had also been the first Warden of one of the new short-term residential colleges for adults established in the UK – Urchfont Manor. He later made a notable contribution to development studies, but he was never a supporter of *university* adult education, especially in Africa.[6]

The Hunters were asked to survey feasibility and to report on all the curricular and administrative aspects of running a citizenship college. Their Report was 'a thorough piece of work' in the judgement of Paul Wangoola (1980). 'It reinforced the need for citizenship colleges; substantiated the existence of support among employers and Government, as well as the existence of an adequate pool of students.'

The Hunters' idea was not so much a single college but 'a system of multiracial education'. The students were to be 'westernised' individual farmers, plus government servants and trainees already about to take responsible jobs in the modern economy. This rising African and Asian middle class could be matched by an increasing number of young Europeans. Altogether they calculated there were something in excess of 25,000 potential candidates for the kind of citizenship education then envisaged. Thus the Capricorn philosophy was maintained in this Report: at the same time, solid practical groundwork had been undertaken for the establishment of an adult education college once the management and philosophy were re-directed.

Two aspects of the Hunters' Report should be noted for their significance in the 1990s. First, that they envisaged a network of colleges or educational programmes rather than one fixed institution, and, second, their insistence on independence from government with finance coming from the private sector.

However, the decision which most influenced the direction the College would take in practice was the appointment of Harold Wiltshire as Principal-designate, and the changes in policy which resulted from his familiarisation tour in May 1960. Wiltshire was already Head of one of the largest university adult education departments in the UK; *inter alia*, this was to give the new college educational respectability at a time when it could have been immersed in a miasma of conflicting and confusing political ideas. And it eventually paved the way for an early link with the University of East Africa and ultimate absorption of the College by the then University College of Nairobi. Moreover, Wiltshire had other characteristics which were to prove decisive. He represented the 'social purpose' tradition of university adult education.

Wiltshire had worked with unemployed mineworkers before moving to a university post and was one of those who made the connection between working class emancipation in the UK in the early twentieth century and the emancipation of east Africans in the 1960s. Above all, he was a considerable scholar who was much more interested in appropriate and high quality teaching than he was in research. As a director he was usually both stimulating and tolerant. But where there was any question of neglect of teaching duties he could be ruthlessly intolerant.

He was also politically astute. Only a year after Lord Kilmaine was asserting that Dulverton had 'snatched' the College from Capricorn, Wiltshire began to plan for changes in the curriculum and admissions policy of the College which would carry it forward for the next decade as a key element, not in 'multi-racial education' but in the Africanisation programme both of Government and of private industry. In terms of our analytical framework, he was already making judgements about changing needs (condition 1) and revising the proposed curriculum in anticipation of participants rather different from those envisaged by the Hunters. Moreover, his familiarisation visit to Nairobi in May 1960 (prior to taking up office in September) came at a crucial time in the changing political fortunes of Kenya. Many African leaders, including Jomo Kenyatta, were still in detention or in exile, but it was by then clear to most outside observers that the future of Kenya (as of Uganda and Tanganyika) would be as a mainly African country.

Independence had not yet been formally achieved, but it was about to be. This did not stop some more blinkered observers failing to read the signs. One distinguished visitor (a British General) who should have known better, told the Principal as late as August 1963 that he hoped he was 'telling these chaps not to ask for independence too soon'! (The colonial regime lasted another four months.)

The wider polity

It is an argument which runs throughout this book that civic education of the kind provided by the College of Social Studies must at least be tolerated by the wider polity if it is to be sustained; in the modern nation state, that state must remain at the minimum a passive stakeholder in the enterprise (condition 3 in our framework). In 1960 power was about to pass to the African majority. The squabbling between various European factions which had seemed so significant only two years before now began to be, if not yet irrelevant, at least of greatly reduced importance. What was urgently necessary was that the College should at least have the tolerant acceptance of African leaders if not yet their enthusiastic support.

An analysis of three key documents from April and May 1960 shows how sudden and dramatic was the shift in attitudes and policy brought about by Wiltshire's appointment and exploratory visit. These documents are: Guy Hunter's personal brief to Wiltshire of 19 April about the important people he should see while in Nairobi; a letter from the Board of Governors inviting recipients to a Conference on 7 May; and the 14 May Report by Wiltshire to the Dulverton Trust.

The Hunter brief now seems significant for what it did not say. All the 'people to see', and for whom thumbnail sketches were provided, were Europeans. Some were included because they had contacts with Asians or Africans, including the Makerere extra-mural resident tutor, Ieuan Hughes (later, Principal of Coleg Harlech in Wales). Much was made of the Capricorn issue and nothing at all of the new political forces then emerging. Some local figures (Sir Philip Rogers, for example) sensed the importance of the coming changes. Many (including the then Chair of Governors, WJD Wadley) did not.

The Chairman's invitation letter announced that the purpose of the Conference was to explain to leading representatives of the community the aims of the College. In addition to the Chairman and Harold Wiltshire, four Legislative Council members were offered as speakers, including two Africans who were Ministers: Dr JG Kiano and Musa Amalemba – the latter a Governor of the College.

It is not clear now whether Dr Kiano was announced as a speaker before his consent had been given, or whether he changed his mind at the last minute. However, on 28 April he wrote to the Chairman that, 'I am not personally convinced that the aims of such a College can be achieved by teaching in classrooms . . . . this is the College that was conceived by the Capricorn Society whose aims and political tactics somewhat differ from mine.' He went on to say that he would not speak at the Conference and that he thought the money would be better spent on building a secondary school. During his visit, it was Wiltshire who convinced Dr Kiano that the College was benign as far as African nationalism was concerned. (This was also very important for the second Principal, Paul Fordham, who had to mediate a potentially explosive racial incident in the first month of his appointment.) Wiltshire also made contact with another key nationalist figure, Tom Mboya, a former student of Ruskin College, Oxford and subsequently a firm supporter of the College until his assassination in 1969.

Wiltshire's Report was forthright on the question of political support:

> *I cannot state too strongly my conviction – confirmed by everyone with whom I talked – of the importance of securing the confidence and support of African leaders. Without this the College cannot have any future . . . All the associations of the College were from this point of view unfavourable . . . .*

He was also forthright on the question of image.

> *The words 'multi-racial' and 'citizenship' should disappear from the title and description of the College. I am persuaded that to African ears, 'College of Citizenship' must sound very much like 'College of Obedience' or 'College of Good Behaviour'; any institution with such a name, sponsored and financed by Europeans, must suggest an attempt to impose upon Africans those concepts of citizenship which are convenient to the European minority. The term, 'multi-racial', too, must in this context imply a last ditch attempt to retain some shreds of privilege for European (and Asian) minorities . . .*

Wiltshire's own suggestion of a title – College of Social Studies – was accepted as sufficiently neutral and simply descriptive of the intended curriculum.

Sustainability and the pre-history of the College of Social Studies: needs, mission and control

At this stage, only the first three conditions in the analytical framework were important. But all three had changed during the brief period of two years during which the College had been planned and the first Principal appointed. At other times and in other contexts, change will seldom be so rapid. But similar processes are likely to be at work wherever adult education programmes are being planned.

First, the needs as defined by the Hunters had now moved away from the list of potential participants they had so carefully enumerated and who were deemed by the founders to be in need of education for citizenship. 'Citizenship' education had not quite disappeared (in a general sense this was what British adult educators of that time were in business to provide); but it had gone from the title and had certainly been re-defined, if only implicitly. 'Nation building' was still a politically acceptable alternative, but it was not uppermost in the minds of those now in charge. What was new and more acceptable all round was the emphasis on enhancing opportunities for the underprivileged African majority. Employers, both public and private, wanted to 'Africanise' as quickly as possible. Education in the social studies could and would be part of this process. This was still to be the kind of education which *could* be for citizenship or for nation building. It was not narrowly vocational. But it was certainly to become part of the vocational training packages which employers were beginning to plan for their upwardly mobile African staff. And it did provide a unique opening into formal education for a few of the many individual applicants who sought it.

Secondly, the mission had changed very substantially. The College of Kenya Citizenship Association (1958) argued that the purpose of the College was 'to show that in our country people of different colour, religion, and culture and people from the countryside and the town can by understanding their spiritual and material dependence on each other, achieve a common sense of national purpose.' The mission statement was never re-written but already by 1960 it had been abandoned and replaced by something implicit and which was derived largely from UK experience. University adult education in 1961 still sought to cater mainly for the underprivileged (in UK parlance the 'workers', Africans in this context), it sought to promote a wider democracy and economic advancement, and it attempted to educate a new leadership cadre by offering opportunities for individual advancement. But this new mission, essentially a cultural transplant from Europe, was always implicit and never publicly debated.

Interestingly, a man who was to become one of the leading politicians in Kenya and a sometime Vice President was already arguing for a largely instrumental and vocational emphasis in 'Education for National Development'. He made a brief obeisance to education as enabling a man 'to be better aware of his universe and thus be enabled to develop and realise himself more fully'; but he also laid great emphasis on 'education as a social (or even economic) investment from which society should expect and get its money's worth'.[7] As in all other countries, education was to be seen increasingly as an investment rather than a consumption good.

Thirdly, the new controlling authorities (the politicians, the civil service and the Board of Governors) were now much happier with the new mission implicit in all the discussions they had had with the new Principal. When the time came, they would be happy to allocate some Government funds to the running of the College, although most of the cash was to come from private foundations for several years to come.

The conditions for sustaining adult education programmes are seldom static, but they can hardly have moved more rapidly than they did in this particular case. However, what all programme designers have to bear in mind is that they may do so. All practitioners need to keep options for change and survival in mind.

Flexible responses to change from the first Principal meant that the stage was set for the building and opening of the new College ready for its first intake of students in August 1961. The photograph of the opening ceremony (see below, p48) still reveals a predominantly European management and sponsorship; but the student body was, from the start, almost wholly African.

Apart from the present writers, the only other analysis of those early days was that undertaken by Paul Wangoola in 1980. His conclusion remains pertinent:

> *When the College of Social Studies opened in June 1961 it may not have enjoyed the support of the nationalist political parties or the labour movement, but it did not suffer from their hostility either.*

The College as it then developed was very much in the image of liberal adult education as developed in the UK and interpreted by Harold Wiltshire and his successor. It is this which forms the substance of the next chapter.

Notes:

[1]Stirling D 1957
[2]Colonial Office 1948 : 12
[3]Quoted in Titmus and Steele, 1995: 19
[4]Colonial Office 1948: 34–35
[5]Wangoola 1980
[6]Hunter 1969
[7]Kibaki 1962

Chapter 3

A cultural transplant takes root

This chapter is first about what kind of institution finally emerged in June 1961 and, second, the contemporary socio-economic, educational and political context in which this took place.

Setting up

The new College was different in many ways from the place (or places) envisaged in 1958, where a common multi-racial citizenship was to be forged. Capricorn remained only in the person of the architect, Richard Hughes*, who, in close consultation with the Principal, designed a simple but elegant building which proved to be an ideal environment for the creation of the sort of learning atmosphere which maximised opportunities for intensive study by heterogeneous groups of adult students.

It was essentially collegiate; the buildings both embraced and enclosed the residents, and made it easy to encourage close interaction between students, and between them and the resident staff. Sited on land donated by the Church of Scotland at Kikuyu, and well away from the counter-attractions of the city, the College provided 30 (extended to 60 in 1963) residential places, initially for three-week problem-centred short courses which discussed the socio-economic and political problems of east Africa – Kenya, Uganda, Tanganyika and Zanzibar.

Wiltshire himself argued that the design of the buildings created its own discipline. As he put it:

> *We banked upon discipline and style . . . The atmosphere of the College was, our visitors told us, friendly and relaxed. It was to a very great extent the influence of the building and of a plan of study and domestic routine which were set out in detail and adhered to without fuss.*[1]

This typically mild comment understates both his own discipline and also his total commitment to the best possible teaching. His gentle warning to his successor – 'You'll find I've become a bit of a disciplinarian here, Paul' – was all he ever claimed for himself.

*True to his own principles, Richard Hughes became the first and only 'European' student to attend a short course at the CSS

Once the College was open, the Governors faded into the background. Most of them were more interested in the political or economic influence their sponsorship might bring, rather than what kind of education they had brought to Kenya; in practice very few of them took a close interest in the College as a teaching institution. They offered support by ensuring that local industry and commerce sponsored students on the courses; but, for the rest, were content to leave the Principal to run the College without supervision, let alone interference. Wiltshire recorded that he found himself 'wholly free to plan the work of the College as I thought fit and to decide what should be taught, how it should be taught and who should teach it.'[2] This freedom continued until the political environment became less open in the late 1960s, and there also began to be more control by the University (of which the College became part in 1963).

The objectives of the College were given their final definition in July 1960. The possibilities were still wide ranging (see Appendix1) but in practice the initial curriculum was determined by the Principal and the staff who were initially appointed to assist him; these were a political scientist appointed from the UK and a local economist recently returned from study at Uppsala in Sweden. The Principal had funds to appoint only two academic assistants and decided that a problem-centred curriculum at that time required economics and political science as its core subjects. He himself would teach race relations within a sociological framework.

What Wiltshire did quite simply was to import the kind of education he knew best, from his experience of university adult education at Nottingham. In a sense, there was nothing new about educational transplants from other cultures. Formal schools and universities in the whole of sub-Saharan Africa are transplants which have been modified over time to suit local circumstances. But there were two aspects of this transplant which were unusual.

First, university adult education in the UK was strongly rooted in its time and place. It was designed to be, and in many respects in the early 1960s still was, civic education on the issues of the day for those social groups who, in the early 1920s, were but recently entitled to vote. In Wiltshire's mind it was still primarily for 'workers' or, as a 1970s writer might have said, for the 'disadvantaged'. Now in the formal school system there are bound to be close similarities between, say, a class in chemistry in Uganda and one in England. But the study of a social science topic in adult education has to start from adult experience; and that experience was vastly different for the people of east Africa and the people of the UK. It is true that east Africans were about to be newly enfranchised in newly created political systems; but the knowledge and understanding they themselves brought to education were different, both in culture and experience. From this perspective the transplant might have been thought likely to fail.

However, the second unusual aspect was Wiltshire's clarity of vision, both about the essential elements of any education for responsible leadership and about the methods which his own experience told him had worked with unschooled adults in the past. Thus, this was an unusual transplant, in that it was established by someone who had himself thought through the theoretical underpinning of what he so successfully practised in the UK; and who now brought this same understanding and applied it in a new context, but with students whose limited experience of schooling was shared with their British counterparts, whatever the cultural and other contextual differences.

Moreover, his depth of understanding also led to a welcome flexibility and willingness to adapt. When confronted with students of unusual ability his immediate reaction was to put on a different kind of course (but with a similar curriculum) which would take them as quickly as possible into regular undergraduate study. So, as well as taking charge of the first year of short courses, he also planned the long course, which was begun when Paul Fordham took over in 1962.

The parallels which Wiltshire drew between the social condition of England in the late 19th/early 20th centuries and east Africa in the early 1960s do not really stand up to close examination (see below) but both his theoretical understanding of what he was doing and his practical good sense as an adult educator were the basis for whatever success was later achieved by the College.

The short-course curriculum

In selecting a social science curriculum, Wiltshire gave two reasons:

> *Any people undergoing a process of economic, political and social change . . . must learn to understand and control it as well as to suffer it. Second, these are the studies which are most appropriate to adults since they are the studies for which experience of affairs is at least as valuable a preparation as classroom study.*

He also went on to note that in short courses there would have to be rigorous selection and limitation of topics 'appropriate to the time and place: in economics, problems of growth in an underdeveloped economy; in politics, problems of establishing a constitution in a new country; in sociology, problems of racial and tribal relations in a mixed community.' This was the overall intention; but the students themselves raised other issues such as land use, party organisation, and communism – which were also incorporated.

> *We had always to try to base our teaching on real East African problems and to help our students analyse these with the tools of the economist, the political theorist or the sociologist.*

He also emphasised that the College did not seek to teach subjects or to produce economists or sociologists:

> *We were trying to help men and women . . . citizens, to see problems more clearly, realise their inter-connections and think straight about them. We could not say: "We will consider the economics of this but we will not consider its political aspects or its social implications". We had no choice but to do all three together, making it clear nevertheless that converging on this problem*

> *were three (or more) different disciplines with different assumptions and different methods of analysis.*

His account of the learning/teaching routine is accurate and vivid; it was a demanding routine for both staff and students alike. It lasted throughout most of the 1960s and its breakdown was one of the elements which contributed to the decline of the College as initially established.

> *We had to work our students very hard indeed. The normal day consisted of three hours teaching in the morning, private study, essay writing, etc., in the afternoon, two hours teaching before dinner, and sometimes a visiting speaker after dinner. We worked through one weekend out of two. At least one essay and other less demanding exercises had to be written each week, and these necessitated steady reading and regular use of the library. It did not surprise us that lights in the study-bedrooms were often burning late . . . . Most of the teaching was done in tutorial groups of about eight . . . All essays were discussed with students individually.*
>
> *What we were offering was, in fact a short period of intensive intellectual training . . . The problems with which we were dealing often aroused strong feelings and touched on deep convictions in students and tutor alike. It was our job to see that these feelings and convictions were made explicit so that they could be brought into the arena of rational discussion. In addition to the existing political and communal passions a respect for facts and a passion for truth were needed. No one can experience this respect and passion without undergoing an educational experience which is moral as well as intellectual.*[3]

The demanding nature of the routine is confirmed by the short-course experience of Patrick Muzaale:

> *There was tremendous pressure. You would have a lecture. Then you would be told to put your books away and have an exam: straightaway. At the end of it you would have an assignment to take to your study-bedroom. I remember spending all the nights – I don't remember sleeping for more than an hour – just enjoying myself reading. The books were so plentiful. I had never come across so many books in my life . . . I was so happy just reading greedily and writing the essays. I went away wondering what would happen if I didn't succeed.*

The routine was also very demanding for staff. The only staff members – two of them, in fact – to be dismissed or asked to resign throughout the 1960s, went because their personal agendas gave priority to things other than the professional culture established very early on: that nothing must interfere with the primacy of the teaching function. Roger Leys, one of the early tutors and interviewed in 1995, points to some of the difficulties in creating this kind of professional culture:

> *I have taught university here for 22 years at the University of Copenhagen, politics and third world studies. I have taught elsewhere and never in my life*

> *have I met students with such motivation and such maturity and such life experience . . . These students were friends, they were not students as I later came to regard university students . . .*

A small collegiate community such as the one established at Kikuyu can only survive on the basis of common purposes and a closeness of living and working together which has many of the characteristics of an extended family. At its best, this can and should produce friendship and dedicated hard work. But we should also be under no illusions that it can also produce tensions and conflicts that interfere with educational goals, especially if the latter are no longer shared by all the teaching staff.

It was noted earlier that there was no new mission statement which explicitly replaced the one originally devised by Capricorn. In the rapidly changing political circumstances of the time, it certainly suited the first two Principals to work to a style and curriculum they knew well, and which all the early tutors shared, rather than to monitor and debate the College purposes and the objectives of the curriculum as the courses developed. But the fact that these were not made explicit did cause tensions in the later 1960s as new staff were appointed.

Students and their assessment

In the first year (1961–62) about 180 people, all men and almost all Africans, mostly between the ages of 25 and 35, attended short courses at the College. About half these students were sponsored by private industry and by Government departments, and half were self-sponsored when they responded to newspaper advertisements or word-of-mouth knowledge. Selection was by staff scrutiny of a written essay, plus the two criteria of 'about' five years of post-school experience and competence in English. In the following year there was a similar number of students, including a homogeneous course of the Kenya Government's graduate administrative trainees from the Kenya Institute of Administration.

Excluding this special course, student occupations broke down as follows:

- clerical 56
- teaching 43
- junior managers 24 (Most sponsored from private sector employers)
- others 31

As Paul Fordham wrote in 1964,

> *The majority of our students were clerks and teachers. People who have had enough education to want more, enough education to speak reasonably good English, but not enough to secure very well paid jobs. They are not the educationally underprivileged of east African society but the educationally ambitious. They want useful skills and the better jobs they hope those skills will bring . . .*[4]

And there was a notable absence of the 'westernised' farmers that the Hunters had envisaged.

Now although the College had set out to do no more than provide a short but intensive intellectual training, the nature and motivation of the students who were recruited led to early decisions and policy changes in two important areas. The first concerned the one or two students of outstanding intellectual ability who were recruited to almost every course, and the second was a recognition of the strong vocational motivation of almost all the students.

The presence of outstandingly able students led directly and immediately to proposals for the long (one academic year) course, while the second led to the creation of a careful system of assessment. The long course is dealt with more fully in the following chapter; but acceptance of the need for rigorous assessment, while it may seem obvious to the modern reader, was such a departure from the 'non-vocational' tradition of British university adult education that it ranks not only as the earliest departure from the academic culture which had been imported, but also the most important in terms of the eventual benefit to students. However, it was an unusual kind of assessment in several important respects. What it attempted was not so much to assess achievement – in the normal three-week course format this would have been very difficult – but rather to make judgements about potential.

The College was never in the business of measuring one student against another, and there were no formal examinations; these would have destroyed the whole basis of recruitment and teaching which assumed a student body of varied ability and background. Each student received a Certificate of Attendance which showed in some detail the work which had been done, including the areas of study; but it did not show grades or marks. Nevertheless, the College did keep 'a careful record of the marks given during the course and these formed the basis of a report which was supplied only on the request of the student himself or of his employer if he had been sent in the employer's time and at the employer's expense.'

These reports were profiles of individual students, and any report sent to an employer was also copied to the student concerned. This use of student profiles was a pragmatic response by academic staff unused to *any* kind of assessment, but who were required by the new context to make a positive effort to meet student and employer demands. It should be recalled that at this time in the UK any idea that university adult education classes should assess students was frowned on by the providing institutions; certification, and a growing variety of assessment procedures, came largely in the 1970s and 1980s.

The College refused to make judgements about an individual's character or qualities of leadership, as these qualities were certainly only imperfectly revealed in a short period of intellectual training. What the reports did contain was:

> *. . . something about ability to grasp concepts and follow argument in the fields in which we were teaching, about powers of expression, about diligence and perseverance and sometimes about range and direction of interest. The basis for this was the record of a student's marks throughout the course and over as wide a range of exercises as possible – including usually at least three essays, two comprehension exercises, two "objective" tests and class discussion . . . At*

the end of the course they were compared and discussed . . . The assessment that resulted . . . could often reveal ability where it had been unnoticed or, less often, the lack of it where it had been assumed . . .[5]

As with the selection of students, which did not depend upon formal qualifications, this kind of assessment was also independent of such qualifications. But it did depend on using an agreed marking convention and on careful and corporate staff analysis after the course had been concluded.

The academic culture of the imported 'Great Tradition'

Only four years before coming to Kenya, Wiltshire had published what many consider to have been his most important and influential essay: *The Great Tradition in University Adult Education*, in 1956. He was talking largely from his experience as Director of the Nottingham Adult Education Department and the kind of educational work with adults which had already been imported into west Africa, and shortly afterwards into east Africa, as 'extra-mural' studies. (To Uganda in1953, Kenya in 1956, and Tanganyika and Zanzibar in 1960.)

A recent analysis of African university extra-mural departments concludes that – eventually – the modifications made to this particular cultural transfer made it worthwhile:

They established structures and practices, solid enough to survive, flexible enough to develop without fundamental damage to themselves, so that the departments of university adult education in both West and East Africa are, for the most part, recognisably the descendants of those set up in the 1950s.

Whether or not one accepts this view, it does beg the question of whether or not the structures and practices were a necessary pre-condition for what those departments have achieved over the last forty and more years. What concerns us here are three areas of extra-mural thinking and practice which are also germane to the early days of the CSS. These are: the notion of university standards, the assertion that such studies should be non-vocational, and the acceptance that education for leadership (or responsibility or citizenship) was not just for the few but could be extended to leadership at all levels of society (as it had been with working class students in the UK).

In the African context, and in the years immediately prior to independence, there was little conflict between these three aspects of extra-mural activities. University standards and a university presence were seen as necessary if classes were to 'foster . . . the growth of an informed outlook, the respect for facts, the development of the critical faculty and the habits of straight thinking.'[6] which were to ensure that newly enfranchised African leaders were to have a 'firm grasp on the distinction between education and propaganda'.[7]

As long as the students came from amongst those described by Robert Gardiner for Nigeria as 'active members of various movements for self-government', they had no need of studies leading to certificates and other paper qualifications. These early students had already been schooled at least to secondary level, and often held degrees as well. Their chosen vocation was politics and many were, or became, the political leaders of the newly independent states. The political and social science curriculum of the new extra-mural studies suited them very well. If it was thought to be 'non-vocational', that was acceptable to them. It certainly helped in their chosen political vocation and the university connection protected free debate from those government officials or special branch officers who thought the whole process subversive.

Assumptions about the educability of ordinary but undereducated people, within a non-formal adult education system, were not really tested until after independence had been achieved. By then the original extra-mural students had moved into politics or other senior public sector jobs, and had been replaced by those eager for preferment in the jobs market place; which preferment they saw as coming in part from the acquisition of paper qualifications.

The students who came to the new College were motivated by a desire for personal advancement rather than a desire for social or political change.* Change was happening very rapidly, Africans were being promoted into positions where they had not yet been tested and for which employers believed they had not yet been trained. Whether they were sponsored by industry or government, or had simply applied on their own account, they could no longer be thought of as 'non-vocational' or interested mainly in social or political purposes. Of course, as adults living in those changing times, they were extremely interested in discussing the social, political or economic issues of the day. But nobody could have been under any illusion that they were doing so for some disinterested concern for social progress. What they wanted was to get on in the world as they saw it, and to take advantages of the new opportunities then opening up. These were the circumstances in which Wiltshire set about trying to transfer to Kenya the ideas he had so recently elaborated in his Great Tradition paper. What then were these ideas and how were they modified to suit new cultural and social circumstances?

The paper describes five main characteristics of the tradition which was transferred: it was committed to a humanities curriculum; its purpose was 'not in learning for learning's sake but in learning as a means of understanding the great issues of life . . .'; it asserted the importance of equality of opportunity; it demanded a 'non-vocational attitude'; and the Socratic method was usually in evidence. This tradition had been clarified and honed in the special circumstances of UK university adult education (or 'extra-mural') departments during the 1920s and 1930s and was carried through to adult education in the British armed forces during World War II. It informed the thinking of those whom the Colonial Office appointed to plan post-war higher education developments in the then colonies.

The origins of the tradition are complex and quite specific to the industrial society from which it sprang. If it was a 'movement' rather than a service (which its adherents claimed) its purpose was to emancipate a whole class of persons who had recently been enfranchised. This class wanted emancipation certainly;

*The evidence for this statement will be found in Chapters 5 and 6.

but they also wanted to be part of an existing developed society (as well perhaps as to modify it), but from which they had hitherto been excluded. But east Africa had not yet developed a society which was stratified into social classes. The racial stratification of the colonial period was thought by some educators at the time to offer similar challenges. They saw themselves as missionaries in the emancipation of Africans. Paul Fordham recalls his own embarrassment when a well meaning visitor assumed his main motivation to be 'to reverse the colonial process'. It would have been an arrogant assumption to believe that a small College could or should have achieved anything so far reaching. What it could do was to help the students who came to understand better their own situation and to change it in ways that they themselves determined. The early staff were all against colonial rule and the inequalities which accompanied it. They *were* part of African de-colonisation. But they did not assume they could or should play a significant political role.

In the later 1990s, development planners are used to asking key questions about any new educational programme: for whom should it be provided; for what purposes; what kind of programme is appropriate and with what methods should it be planned and implemented? For the Great Tradition, these questions had been answered as early as 1919 in a UK government report about state-supported adult education. It was for 'workers'; it was to promote and enhance the effectiveness of a wider democracy and to contribute to national economic regeneration; it was civic education (public education on the issues of the day for participation in public life and the leadership of newly enfranchised social groups) and to succeed it would require 'fostering and special methods of teaching'.[8]

If 'Africans' is substituted for 'workers', then this and the preceding paragraphs give a fair summary of the corpus of ideas which Wiltshire imported to the new College at Kikuyu. But these ideas were, of course, placed in a totally different context – and it is unsurprising that modifications soon had to be made. However, what is surprising is that the early modifications were so few, concentrating as they did on only one of the five characteristics: the non-vocational attitude.

From the 1920s onwards, university adult education in the UK took over the view, predominant in the University of Oxford, that a university education should be for rigorous intellectual training or even for an active and informed citizenship; but it should not be utilitarian. Only in this way was it possible to engage in free and open debate, or adopt a dialogical pedagogy with full learner participation both in class discussion and in design of curriculum.

Now in many discussions in the Nottingham University common room, Wiltshire had always made clear that what he called the 'Great' tradition was also the 'Greats' tradition of the University of Oxford: the study of subjects which could never be described as instrumental except for scholars (the classics, or for 'modern Greats' the social sciences and humanities), and in a way which gave a rigorous intellectual training without specific vocational outcomes in mind.

What it did do, of course, was to prepare students better both for leadership and for subsequent vocational training. What Wiltshire preserved at Kikuyu was the Oxford methodology and curriculum: what he very quickly moved to change was the commonly accepted definition of non-vocational. Almost everything else had transplanted rather well.

What was referred to earlier as the 'Nottingham' approach had itself come from an institution (the University of Oxford) with very different purposes – the non-vocational education of a ruling elite. But this did not exclude the subsequent exercise of leadership and responsibility in the wider society. The Oxford tutorial system, via Nottingham and the practice of a modified adult education tradition that he introduced, was what lay behind Wiltshire's success at Kikuyu. However, in looking at the success of curriculum and method throughout the 1960s, we should not underestimate the influence of adult education seen as a social and reformist movement.

The motivation of many expatriate members of staff lay in contributing to African liberation from colonial rule and the mental shackles which accompany it. Tom Mulusa (a tutor in the late 1960s) links this with previous experience in trying to eliminate social class disadvantage in the UK when he describes a former colleague (Leslie Stephens) as coming from the 'right' background. This new kind of missionary zeal was important; but it was implanted into a very different economic, social and educational context, in spite of the parallels which the founders tried to draw.

The east African context

In the mid-1960s an analysis was made of the possibilities of modernisation and economic growth in Africa which points clearly to the danger of drawing too close a parallel between nineteenth century England and the east Africa of that decade.

In England, economic development and a complex division of labour had been the sources of the rise to power of whole new social classes; and these classes were embedded in an existing and interlocking web of established institutions. In Africa the reality was quite different. Here, a 90 per cent rural and subsistence economy had had grafted onto it within living memory a very small and still largely alien polity and economy. Independence saw the rise of young and educated Africans into positions of power within this small modern economy and administration. But this was a one-off leap forward by those few who were in the right place at the right time. Further economic and social development took place over the next thirty years from this very small and (as Uganda under Amin was to show) very fragile base of the modern economy. Guy Hunter (1967) makes a comparison between east Africa and England, by surveying the crafts and skills available to the rural 90 per cent and asks which century would we choose as equivalent to 1960s Africa. Would it be 1750?

> *England was immensely more developed. 1650? The same is still true. Apart from agriculture there was a coal industry, a metallurgical industry, a woollen industry spread over great regions of the country, exporting to Europe and America . . . shipbuilding, glass and a dozen other manufactures . . . a huge*

array of rural crafts associated with agriculture and transport; a great class of merchants and a merchant marine . . . a view of England in 1688 lists 400,000 middle class (doctors, lawyers, civil servants, officers, merchants, etc.), 225,000 shopkeepers, 240,000 artisans, all lying below the upper classes (125,00 large freeholders, 30,000 squires and above them the nobility, the upper clergy, the Court). All this was in a population of $5\frac{1}{2}$ million, smaller than that of Uganda today . . .[9]

However, there are limits to the comparative value of this cautionary description. First there is no identification of the crafts and skills of rural east Africa, such as pottery, blacksmithing or thatching. Moreover, Uganda also had its nobility, upper clergy and several courts. There were also great differences in access to it. Modern technology and communication systems have affected all societies, and twentieth century people, whether in Europe or Africa, live in a totally different way from their predecessors.

Any such comparison must also be accompanied by the recognition that as well as a small modern economy, colonial rule had also brought a modern educational system – and an increasingly sophisticated system of communication. The higher education apex was still very small; but the very rapid increases in enrolments in primary and junior secondary education throughout the 1960s meant a growing group of school leavers looking for further education. It was the adults from this group that the CSS came to recruit. When in the late 1960s this group became so large that the higher education system could not take all of the younger leavers with 'A' level entry qualifications, the Kenya Government decided it could manage without education at Kikuyu for older adults. But this is to anticipate the main thrust of our Chapter seven.

A flying start

In terms of recruitment, the College was an instant success. Employers were happy to sponsor candidates onto the short courses, and recruitment of individuals by press advertisement overwhelmed the one office clerk who had been appointed. So much was this the case, that when the second Principal took over (August 1962) he found a drawer full of unopened mail, most of it from eager would-be students.

Money was tight, in spite of generous support from the Carnegie Corporation, and the small size of the staff which could be afforded certainly limited the curriculum which could be offered. But although this meant that curriculum relevance had to be carefully monitored, it also meant a tight intellectual and ideological cohesion amongst the teaching staff. Part of this was Wiltshire's own disciplinary code (taken over by his successor) that the teaching function must always take precedence over other legitimate interests. The only staff member to leave in the early days did so because he chose to ignore this code.

Former students pay tribute to the influence of the library. As a learning resource it was well chosen and well used. It helped to open windows onto worlds beyond student experience, as well as illuminating those with which they were familiar. One of the early students thought it was too small, but it grew very rapidly in the first five years of the College's operation. The building itself was also a learning resource. Its design reinforced the collegiate atmosphere and helped the teaching staff to develop an informal but disciplined style of teaching.

With each new course, the latter took time to establish. Most students only had experience of very formal school teaching. One early technique was to dress smartly (collar and tie for sure) on the first half day and to give a few formal lectures, just to establish credibility. After that, it was time to give due weight to students' own experience and understanding, which they tended to undervalue.

It is the argument of this book that both the general education for citizenship or civic/social responsibility of the short courses and the provision of access to higher education for very able adults which was later developed in the long course (see the next chapter) are both desirable elements in the educational provision of any country, whatever its demographic circumstances or the size of its educational budget. All countries need good quality leadership and no country can afford to waste the scarce talent of the exceptionally able. But to ensure that the proposed long course did in fact ensure access to university, it now seemed necessary to bring a new stakeholder onto the Kikuyu campus – the University of East Africa and its then University College of Nairobi – which eventually became the independent University of Nairobi.

Notes:

[1]Wiltshire 1963 : 73–74
[2]Wiltshire 1963 : 70–71
[3]Wiltshire 1963 : 75–76
[4]Fordham 1964
[5]Wiltshire 1963 : 74
[6]Titmus and Steele 1995 : 111
[7]Colonial Office 1948 : 34
[8]Wiltshire et al : 1980
[9]Hunter 1967 : 7

Chapter 4

Access, the university connection and the one-year course

The University as stakeholder

The university connection began because of the background of the first two Principals in university adult education on the UK model; but it was cemented by the need to ensure that the proposed one year course would indeed lead to university entrance. Whereas former students, from the perspective of 1995, did not see the local universities as relevant to any future Kikuyu type adult education programme, both Wiltshire and Fordham saw the university link as both desirable and inevitable. They were used to the special circumstances of the UK at that time, where a university connection gave some protection for the adult education 'mission' from those critics who might wish to alter or ignore it. They did not foresee that sustainability would be threatened once the relations began to change between University and Government, and between the University mission and that of its outreach arm.

Because of their background and previous experience, the two first Principals made assumptions which were certainly not shared by other observers from the UK; observers who were equally sympathetic to the national and personal aspirations of east Africans. For example, a visiting social development adviser from the UK Government in the mid-1960s thought the new University connection a 'mistake', and that the College should be involved more closely with community development. The same Guy Hunter who had reported to the Dulverton Trust a decade earlier was by 1969 extremely critical of the 'extra-mural functions of universities' with which the College at Kikuyu was closely associated. It was more important in his view that resources should be applied to 'very simple' forms of adult education like literacy and basic skills.[1]

Universities have not proved either adept or very interested in promoting these alternatives. Nevertheless, there is a widespread belief in countries that have adopted either a British or an American model of higher education, that universities should do more than engage in undergraduate or graduate teaching and high level research. In most of these countries, and however vaguely expressed, there is or has been a commitment to extending university knowledge to wider publics. In turn, this has given rise to expectations that: there will be increasing access to the universities' store of knowledge through flexible admissions procedures (like mature age entry schemes) and widely based extension or external studies programmes. As we explore in the final chapters, much of late twentieth century external studies, is either post-graduate professional continuing education or various kinds of access programmes for non-traditional entry to undergraduate courses. But in the UK tradition of the 1960s, universities sought to promote a much wider and more diffuse set of programmes. As one highly experienced university adult educator argued in 1970*, 'a university is above all an engine of thought. . .unless it teaches people to *think* clearly, society is doomed'. And she went on to argue that it was acceptable to give students the 'pieces of paper' they wanted as long as in the process they were 'genuinely educated'.

The Colonial Government's stake in promoting a programme of adult education for 'responsible self-government' and 'evolutionary democracy' has already been noted. For the University of East Africa and its constituent colleges, the commitment to extra-mural studies stemmed from the 1940s' policy decision of the British Government to expand higher education in the colonies. High level commissions were established[2]and the acceptance of their Reports by Government led directly to the establishment of new universities like Ibadan (Nigeria) and Makerere (Uganda), initially under the protective wing of the University of London. In all cases, 'extra-mural studies' were recommended as an integral part of university development. This was adult education designed to smooth the path to independence; the political assumption and purpose was clear. Democracy would only work if there were an educated and responsible political leadership, both within active politics and the newly enfranchised electorate. What had been provided in the UK for trades union leaders and newly enfranchised workers in the early twentieth century would now be exported for a similar purpose in Africa. It shared with the Capricornists a certain paternalism, but it was also much more broadly conceived than the simple propaganda which might have been promoted. It was also quite different from the experience of the French colonies, where there was no university adult education tradition and, in the event, very little adult education was ever established there from a university base.

Briefly, the arguments advanced by the British Colonial Office were as follows:

- There are many individuals who had no chance to attend university as full-time students but who have the capacity to benefit from it. University outreach facilities can help to widen access to higher education for such people (also the 'second chance' argument for the long course at Kikuyu);
- Even those few who have received good secondary plus professional or higher education need to keep up to date with new professional and/or subject knowledge if their skills are to be effectively utilised; short refresher courses are therefore essential (the 'continuing education' argument);
- Universities should influence both educational and cultural affairs at all levels in society and this is a two-way process (the widespread intellectual leadership argument);
- In order to retain social cohesion in the exercise of this leadership and to

*Lalage Bown, personal correspondence

prevent the universities becoming a divisive influence, contacts with the wider society should be maximised (the social responsibility argument);
- Universities had a role to play in helping to educate an adult elite in the responsibilities of independence.

This was the mission which the University of East Africa, as providing agency, took over from the Colonial Office, and the first 'resident tutor' appointment was made in 1953 (mainly for Uganda) with a similar appointment following for Kenya in 1956. In view of what happened at Kikuyu in 1968 (the presence of a Special Branch agent in the long course and the arrest of one of the teaching staff – see Chapter 7), it is worth noting that the original mission received only selective acceptance by local civil servants and political leaders. Bernard de Bunsen (first Vice-Chancellor of the University of East Africa) remembered considerable opposition to these early appointments, not just from white settler interests but from civil servants and some missionary headmasters who thought both higher education and its adult education offshoot were dangerous for Africans who weren't ready for a free university life. Even non-revolutionary socialists on the staff were thought to be dangerous. The first resident tutor in colonial Kenya (Ieuan Hughes) told of his exposure of the Special Branch man in his class by ordering: 'will the policeman in the class please stand up!' He did. The Government of independent Kenya did not invent the idea of police informers in education classes. There was always a limit to the tolerance afforded to this kind of programme.

The birth of the long course

Now the chosen university vehicle for 'education for independence' was the programme of extra-mural classes but, as independence approached, the mission which 'for independence' implies, was soon in conflict with the overwhelmingly vocational motivation of students. In the face of official inertia, academic staff had to respond in various ways to this dilemma. They usually stuck to the official line that studies were 'non-vocational', but in practice gave the students what they wanted, often in a disguised form which tried to satisfy both the official policy of the University and the commitment of the tutor to student needs. As Ezekiel Mphahlele described it for Nigeria:

> *I skated very close to GCE requirements. When I smelled trouble, I announced solemnly the need for the students to be initiated into imagery through African speech. . .After tackling James Stephens'* The Shell, *Lorca's* Song of the Barren Tree, *and D H Lawrence's* The Snake *. . . we took a heavy dose of Keats, the GCE prescribed work of the year.*[3]

At Kikuyu, the short courses as originally conceived had a similar mission to the University's extra-mural classes. Similarly, they could only be sustained if the mission of the College was not totally at variance with the motivation of the students. The initial extra-mural response was to modify the curriculum in the direction of an external examination (the GCE): the response at Kikuyu was to offer a new access course and, later, a new public examination (the Certificate of Adult Studies).

Wiltshire had noted right from the start that there was 'in almost every one of our courses one or two students whose intellectual ability was obviously quite outstanding'[4]. And in his first Development Plan (August 1961) he had gone so far as to say that, of the 35 students admitted in June/July 1961 (33 African and two Asian), of these 'certainly four and possibly five could take good degrees in any British university'. He went on to argue that no 'teacher can stand by and see ability of this kind wasted, and no country can afford to allow so much of its intellectual capital to lie unused'. His solutions were twofold: encouragement to employers to offer further training and up-grading; and the 'long course'.

The early terminology was important. The aim was to have the conventional academic year (three terms each of eight weeks), but offered in a much shorter time (seven months) than a calendar year. It was clear that a *full-time* course of this kind would be expensive both in staff time and in the maintenance/family support costs then thought to be necessary as a direct cost to the College. There would be no lengthy vacations, and the rest of the College year was designed to be filled with short courses; these were also to run in parallel with the long course. Significantly, when the College became a university department, this course soon became a 'one-year' course and one which was seen as too expensive to sustain. In one early review, the Professor of Economics described the programme at Kikuyu as 'a very expensive exercise'. But although intensive teaching is always more expensive than less intensive, there was then no recognition that the 'long' course did achieve highly cost effective results for those who completed it. The time was yet to come when universities of the UK type would want to alter structures to make teaching more intensive and/or to save money. Moreover, the College itself modelled the course on the UK pattern for long term residential colleges like Ruskin in Oxford; cheaper multi-media and mixed mode alternatives like the Open University had not yet been conceived.

There was thus a sleight of hand element in the initial planning, designed to circumvent University or other regulations which might withhold recognition from a course that did not offer the full complement of contact hours or the necessary over-all length to be accorded 'one-year' status. Other adult educators have also been adept at finding ways round existing regulations in the interests of mature age students. One later example is the Weekend College and University Studies programme devised at Wayne State University in Detroit in the 1970s. In this case, full time automobile workers were also registered as full-time students in order to capture student motivation and retain ex-veteran's student support.[5]

Numbers in the initial long courses were to be kept very small, both to keep down the costs of student support and to ensure that teaching remained mainly a matter of individual tuition, and of practice in the techniques of study, such as essay writing. The syllabus followed would 'be built round a basic study of History, Economics and Political Theory plus . . .Sociology or Economic Geography or Industrial Relations', but Wiltshire went on to assert, 'this would have to be agreed with the universities concerned'[6]. The University was thus already able to have an influence on the content of the curriculum even before it became formally responsible for it.

In practice, the curriculum content was based on that of the short courses with the addition of a large element of study skills. The social science subjects were determined by the interests of those tutors already in post, together with those of the new history tutor. English, so important an element of the study skills programme, was initially undertaken by locally recruited part-timers like the wife of the second Principal and the English language specialist of the British Council in Nairobi. The initial timetable for the early part of the first long course is instructive: one seminar a week in each of; economics, history, international relations, political science and statistics, plus another weekly seminar on essay writing. The rest of the timetabled periods (making 15 in all) were devoted entirely to individual tutorials. Each student could expect five individual tutorials each week plus other informal contacts with staff in bar and dining room. During the short courses, all students shared in the evening visiting lecturer programme; this included academics, leading politicians, visitors from overseas and senior civil servants who all gave generously of their time.

The aim was to train alert, intelligent and mature people to be students, not to teach specific subject syllabuses. Selection until 1965, was entirely by talent spotting on the short courses. The experiment in that year with a selection examination was probably due to a combination of staff changes and the influence of university practices. From 1967 a selection examination became the norm although, as will be seen, this was accompanied by other significant changes both in curriculum content and in methods of teaching.

Becoming part of the University*

The long course was the main, but only one of six reasons, for seeking to become part of the University. The others were:

- the argument that the work at Kikuyu would have 'higher standing' if attached to the University and that this was supported by the chief donor for the long course (the Ford Foundation);
- it would provide 'a much needed element of continuity' once the foundation staff had been replaced;
- follow-up work from the short courses could be provided by the Extra-Mural Departments;
- a qualification at the end of the long course (in the event the Certificate of Adult Studies) would need University recognition if it were to become established, and perhaps used as part of the training of social workers or community development officers;

*Initially the Royal College, then University College, Nairobi of the University of East Africa: from 1968 the University of Nairobi

- if Government grant came via the University, 'with its independence more strongly entrenched than ours will ever be' then the College would be less open to political pressure if there were to be changes in Government personnel or policy.

Now all these arguments were valid in the country from which they derived (the UK) but, apart from access by mature age entry, they none of them proved valid for east Africa. This is said with the wisdom of hindsight, for neither of the first two Principals would have dissented from any of these arguments at the time. As explored in the final chapters, the invalid assumptions behind these arguments were in part responsible for ensuring that the College (as originally conceived) was not sustainable into the 1970s.

The long course needed the accompaniment of mature age entrance procedures. Already by 1961, Wiltshire had spoken to the Principals of Makerere (Uganda) and Nairobi (Kenya) to secure their agreement to a suitable scheme and in March of the following year, detailed proposals were placed before the University's Academic Committee. The way was now clear for the first mature age entrance examination to be held in 1963.

Unfortunately, however, the process by which the University of East Africa agreed to the Mature Age Entry scheme, showed that the College of Social Studies was regarded with suspicion by the Extra-Mural Department already established at Makerere. In particular, there was already the question of who was to take over whom when a unified Institute of Adult Studies (uniting the College and the Extra-Mural Department), was created. While unimportant in themselves, these essentially personal rivalries, did foreshadow the more important disputes over policy which eventually led to the abandonment of the original College idea.

It was Wiltshire who suggested a scheme of mature age entry, and he did so without any formal discussion with the Head of the Extra-Mural Department in Kampala. This gave rise to a rival proposal, not very different in itself, but which showed the suspicion with which the two Heads (and their supporting staff) then viewed each other. The Registrar, Lindsay Young, had little difficulty in reconciling the two proposals. Briefly, what was agreed was that candidates must be over 25 years of age, have been out of full-time education for at least five years, have attended either extra-mural classes or a residential college or be recommended by some person or authority whose judgement the University was prepared to accept. There was also to be a special examination consisting of a General Paper 'on the model of the HSC General Paper'; and an essay. All this remained the established pattern for mature age entry until the withdrawal of Kenya Government support in 1969. The mature age entry scheme is still operative at Makerere University in Uganda. In Kenya, regulations remain but are not in practice utilised.

One other cultural borrowing suggested by Wiltshire was an elaborate system of governance (A Delegacy for Extra-Mural (or Extension) Studies with two separate governing committees); this would have retained for Kikuyu 'a measure of independence (both in finance and in policy) which it has earned and which it merits'.[7] It was not to be. Two Departments did come into being for a short time, but the then University College saw no reason to tolerate 'a College within a College' and the CSS was soon absorbed into a larger Institute of Adult Studies as the Adult Studies Centre. In moving from CSS to ASC, there was a real loss of independence, although nobody saw this clearly at the time.

Trends and portents

Six years after the establishment of the College and in the fifth year of the long course (1966–67) there were discernible trends away from the intentions of the founders. Many were in part a result of the University connection, although the pressure of student applications, staff changes and increasing authoritarianism in politics all played their part. Three trends referred to here, seem to have particular significance both for the post-1968 decline and for the planning and sustainability of any similar ventures in the future. These are:

- increased student numbers on the long course and a reduced number of short courses;
- a more formal curriculum and teaching methods (more lectures, fewer seminars and tutorials);
- policy changes which emphasised the *university* role in adult education and underplayed the role of the College.

From 1966 onwards there was a rapid increase in long course numbers from 9 to 30. At the same time the number of short courses declined until in 1969 only two were held. It can be inferred from various internal papers that at least one of these courses was a training course for adult educators from voluntary organisations. In the 1968 total of four courses at least one was two weeks extra tuition for candidates wishing to take the Certificate of Adult Studies in English. The long course had now become the main programme at Kikuyu. Access for the few was dominant.

Patrick Muzaale recalls that by 1966 the main method of instruction was the lecture, plus individual tutorials based on the discussion of marked written work; and this then remained the pattern until the end of the decade. In other words the system then adopted resembled more the long established Oxford pattern rather than the closer personal interaction in more frequent tutorials (the 'Nottingham' variant) originally adopted. More significantly, the emphasis in the later 1960s was much more on passing a formal examination in the various subjects of the Certificate of Adult Studies, rather then concentrating on study skills per se; and on increasing student chances in an examination designed to test academic potential. The course still fulfilled these last two objectives, but it did so on the basis of an increasingly formal curriculum.

By 1968 the draft timetable for the first term of the one-year course covered four periods per day (22 in all), of which 15 were lectures. Only one period was set aside for 'Tutorials' with two others as 'Private Study or Tutorials'. In contrast to the first Long Course when all tutorials were timetabled, students were expected to arrange 'individual tutorials' with tutors assigned to them. An internal paper written at the time claimed:

> *the teaching . . . is on the same lines as University teaching with lecture periods interspersed with seminars and individual or small group tutorials.*

But perhaps the 1967 policy statement is most revealing of all about how things were to change and about what further changes were to happen in the future. The statement (see Appendix 2) was written by Paul Fordham at a time when he knew he would be leaving a year later, and because he reflected that between April and September of 1967, he would be the only person on the academic staff who would still be in post. How was continuity to be assured? And what policy would be adopted by his successors? It seemed prudent to set down what present thinking was, even though there was no guarantee that it would be maintained. Apart from Annual Reports (always an opportunity for *ex post facto* justification and blowing one's own trumpet) there was nothing written about what policy then was, let alone what it should or might be. In the 1990s we could hardly have proceeded without a mission statement and the delineation of aims and objectives. In the 1960s we assumed much more, and assumed (wrongly as it turned out) there would usually be a consensus about how to proceed. Nevertheless, Paul Fordham, as the new Director of the Institute of Adult Studies, was worried enough to want to put his ideas down on paper and to have them discussed as much as possible.

Although the statement retains something of the original aims (e.g. making possible more 'effective popular participation in government'), the actual programmes proposed are much more university oriented and much less national development oriented than those of the CSS founders. 'Remedial' education is to be 'at the highest level' with an emphasis on the Certificate examination (no mention of helping citizens or leaders at all levels). 'Continuing' education for decision makers (leadership training) appears for the first time as does the idea of the Institute acing as a service agency for other agencies. This last point opened the way directly for what was to become the main business at Kikuyu in the 1970s: the training of adult education professionals through a Diploma course. Finally, the new Correspondence Course Unit was seen, not as an innovative (and cost effective) way of channelling some of the increasingly insistent demands for more secondary education (the Government's reason for support), but as setting 'new standards of excellence and professional skills in a previously neglected field'. University-speak had taken over from thinking about fundamental purposes! The new stakeholder had become the dominant force, almost by default.

Notes

[1]Hunter 1969 : 294–295
[2]Most notably the Elliot Report 1945
[3]Mphahlele 1963
[4]Wiltshire 1963 : 75

[5]Bertelsen et al 1977
[6]Wiltshire 1961b
[7]Wiltshire 1962

Chapter 5

Students and the Kikuyu experience

Who were the long-course students?

Students' backgrounds are so individual and varied that it is impossible to profile the 'typical student' in other than barest outline. Moreover, gaps in the data, especially for the middle years of 1964–66, are too many to allow a detailed statistical analysis. Nevertheless, certain generalisations can be made from the information assembled on a course by course basis.

These were not the educationally underprivileged of east African societies, but those with a fair to good command of English and enough education to know that more was necessary, both for personal development and for career advancement. As individuals, they would have taken up almost any available opportunity to further their education, and the programme offered at the CSS was only one of many which might have met their 'real need'.

Would some other kind of education have served as well? Certainly an 'Open University' of the UK type might have done something along the same lines, but these did not yet exist. The need at that time was to provide access to those universities which already existed, not to establish an alternative University.

The student analysis (and that of their subsequent career paths in Chapter 6) is based mainly on complete or partial information from 104 of the total of 130 students attending the long course between 1962 and 1969. Additional perceptions are derived from interviews with former members of the teaching staff.

Analysis of student profiles

Educational background

This was the single most important factor which students had in common. The overwhelming majority had been limited to primary and/or junior secondary schooling, usually stopping short of any opportunity to take O levels at school. Some had done so at school, and a few had completed afterwards by private study. None had the A levels then necessary for entrance to the University of East Africa (later the three Universities of Dar es Salaam, Makerere and Nairobi).

Table 5.1: Student numbers 1961–70

Date	Short Courses	Long Course
1961–62	35 students on 2 courses	nil
1962–63	141 on 8	7
1963–64	156 on 8	8
1964–65	143 on 8	8
1965–66	168 on 7	9
1966–67	174 on 6	16
1967–68	68 on 3	25
1968	117 on 4	30
1969	47 on 2	27
1970	13 on 3 mths. course on Ad Ed	0
Totals	**1062**	**130**

Source: Short course statistics from Raphoto D (1971) in paper (unpublished) to African Adult Education Association Annual Conference, 19–24 April on "The Growth and Development of Adult Education at the Adult Studies Centre, Kikuyu"

Long course statistics from pass lists in CSS/ASC Annual Reports and some staff memories for 1964–65 where the Report/list is missing.

The ten for whom no names are available are presumed to have failed both the CAS and Mature Age entry examinations. Including these ten, there is no information on a total of 26 students. Of the remaining 104, there is partial information on 50 former students (of whom 17 are known to have died) and full information on 54 students (one of whom has died since being interviewed). A total of 30 students has been interviewed, either in groups or individually. The detailed statistical information and explanation of survey/interview procedures is at Appendix 3.

Table 5.2: Number of long-course students with no secondary schooling

Course	Total students	Without Sec. School
1962–63	7	5 out of 7
1963–64	8	4 out of 7*
1964–65	8	
1965–66	8	2 out of 3
1966–67	16	3 out of 6
1967–68	25	4 out of 10
1968	30	8 out of 14
1969	27	4 out of 10

*Data from respondents incomplete for this and all subsequent courses.

If further information were to reveal that there was a significant trend towards more students with some secondary schooling, this would not be surprising, as there was rapid secondary school expansion throughout east Africa in the 1960s. Much more significant is the absence of evidence of any correlation between years of schooling and subsequent educational or career success (Fordham, 1966 and see below 'mature entrants as undergraduates').

Some contemporary adult educators were critical of the CSS in that it did not seek to attract the 'underprivileged'. However, it can be argued that, although the students recruited were part of a relatively privileged group (in that the majority of the population then never had any kind of schooling), there were nevertheless elements of relative deprivation which made appropriate the kind of second chance and remedial opportunities then being offered:

- primary and junior secondary schooling was limited in scope and did not make learners part of a reading culture;
- books were not part of the culture of the home, and library facilities few or non-existent;
- students were part of the African majority for whom racial discrimination and third class schooling (in terms of resources), were part of very recent experience;
- the language of education (English) was a second (or third) language for most students and few had sufficient command of it to benefit fully from secondary or higher education without further remedial help;
- other educational opportunities for this level of student were either limited or not available;
- without financial support, no under qualified mature student without private means could hope to enter full-time higher education.

Gender

With three exceptions, all the students were male. While the College would have welcomed more women students, it made no effort to exercise positive discrimination in their favour. Moreover, none of the students sponsored by employers was female and the number of women applying for short course admission was very small.

There is no doubt that this dearth of women students was a clear reflection of prevailing male attitudes. Most women of the normal student age range (mid 20s to mid 30s) would be married and husbands usually unwilling to allow wives to attend a mixed college. The only former woman student available for interview made much of the encouraging attitude of her husband – 'my husband (a university administrator) didn't complain, but he made sure every Friday I was working alone: I usually managed to get home for the weekend'. Nevertheless, she still found life was difficult as a woman student:

> *There are far more hurdles to clear. The opportunities are far less – and you have to prove yourself as tough, if not tougher than men.*

Paul Fordham recalls only two women students who attended entirely on their personal initiative. The first, from Uganda, attended the 1962–63 course and was already a senior figure in various voluntary activities connected with the Church of Uganda, notably the YWCA. The second found she did not need the one-year course to gain the rapid promotion soon achieved in the Ministry of Foreign Affairs; she was and remained unmarried, itself unusual in the local culture.

One former tutor (Sheila Gifford), points out that there was an all female alternative to the CSS. This was the Kenya-Israel School of Social Work established at Machakos. As an independent college it existed throughout much of the same period as the College of Social Studies. Although oriented to a specific vocation, it had the same flexible entry requirements as were current at Kikuyu and attracted the same kind of educationally ambitious student. However, there was no direct encouragement at Machakos to proceed to mature age university entry.

Previous work experience

Superficially, previous employment was almost as homogeneous as educational background. The overwhelming majority for whom information is available were clerks and teachers: 30 of the former and 25 of the latter. Of the 25 teachers, ten remained in school teaching or teacher training (after they left Kikuyu) until their last or penultimate jobs. Another seven persons (for whom early information is missing) were also in teaching or teacher training at the end of their careers (This total of 17 excludes a further 11 students who went into university teaching and administration). Given that only one of the students for whom full information is available went from another job into teaching, we can assume that most if not all of the seven were teachers when they came to the College, making 32 in all out of 62 for whom we have information. Both available statistics and tutor memories would indicate that around half the students came from primary school teaching. There is a parallel here between Kikuyu and the UK Open University's intake of students in the early 1970s, a high proportion of whom were from a similar background. There were also similar criticisms that the OU was not attracting as many of the genuine 'working class' as had been hoped for, although it was also shown that the majority of these students had working class parents. In fact, historically in Britain, teaching, especially primary teaching, was very often the path to upward mobility for able working class men and women because the training was subsidised; the same could be true in Africa.

'Clerical workers' (30) includes those who were sponsored by employers as part of their desire to Africanise junior managerial positions. Special mention must be made of the five railway workers and two chiefs (in Kenya, not a hereditary office but the lowest grade of local civil service appointment). All achieved later distinction in their chosen careers. If we add these to the 30 clerical workers, the total of 36 again indicates that probably around half of the student intake was of this category of worker.

In sum, most of the students came with a background of primary or junior secondary education, and all but three were male. About half were primary school teachers and about half were from a variety of clerical or junior administrative jobs. In the view of the College, all the students selected for the long course had academic potential beyond their contemporary level of formal educational attainment.

The 'mission' of the College and the motivation of students

In the 1990s, such a College would almost certainly have a mission statement, written down and understood by all those who worked and studied there; it would be likely to motivate the efforts of all stakeholders, the staff and students included. However, it was quite evident from discussions with the former staff and students that the formal mission of the college was not then clearly specified. It is true that written and well publicised mission statements were not then considered so important as they are today, certainly not in the British educational system. There was an expectation of shared assumptions and purposes which the first Principal simply transferred to this new setting. However, beyond this, there was the fact that the College had already departed from part of the original mission as conceived by Capricorn. The Secretary of the Dulverton Trust was correct in asserting that the College had been 'snatched' from Capricorn (see Chapter 2). As a result, Harold Wiltshire was none too keen on continuing debate about purposes and preferred to do good (as he saw it), by stealth if necessary. He was committed to African emancipation and advancement. He was committed to Africanisation in employment. The Governors gave him a totally free hand to establish a College well suited to these purposes and he had the foresight to make the crucial addition of the long course; this rapidly became the main goal of the short course students, whether or not they were sponsored by employers or individually recruited by means of advertisements.

The long tradition of civic education in which the College was rooted placed great emphasis on the development of rational thought and analysis as essential pre-conditions of democratic debate and government; according to the founders, this was what was needed if the newly independent states in east Africa were to survive, flourish and develop. Thus 'nation building' rather than individual self advancement was what most of them had in mind. However, the 'rigorous intellectual training' which the first Principal saw as essential to this initial purpose also turned out to be entirely appropriate for the remedial training and later access to higher education which motivated so many of the students actually recruited. When the 'long' course was created to facilitate mature student access, the needs as perceived by the students and those in the minds of the founders all neatly coincided. This, coupled with the fact that local employers (both Government and the private sector) saw the short courses as 'training' for their rapid Africanisation programme gave the College a sense of early success and of mission which such a young institution clearly must have. As far as the students were concerned, it was a good opportunity to gain access to the higher education which most of them wanted.

While the formal mission of the College remained obscure at the time, former staff and students interviewed during 1995–6 were happy to speculate about it. With some variation in detail, all the individual responses of students and teaching staff saw the CSS as having aimed to help students learn about the political, economic, and social affairs of their societies as well as well as enabling individual access to higher education and to improved career prospects. The following purposes were most frequently mentioned: to help develop individual potential; to help develop self-confidence; to open windows onto wider worlds; and to provide opportunities to advance to higher education. In brief, the mission of the college was perceived both by the staff and by the students as having been to do with both national and individual betterment, but with the former a largely incidental effect of the latter. Recruitment was never a problem, except that the number of written applications could sometimes be overwhelming.

Who were the teaching staff ?

Nearly all members of the teaching staff were young men and women in their twenties who had recently graduated from University; for most of them this was either a first or very early teaching experience. Three members of staff came under a six year agreement with the University of Nottingham which from 1964 agreed to second each of them for two year periods. Apart from the Principals, the only more senior staff member was a South African refugee (Picton Mbatha) who had substantial school teaching experience in South Africa and Rhodesia.

Those from the UK came primarily because of an interest in east Africa or knowing about the outside world or because of an interest in the processes of decolonisation. Many had not yet made up their minds about their professional careers, although the series of Nottingham secondments gave an important element of continuity and understanding of the mission pursued by Wiltshire and his successors (Fordham and Stephens). It was near the end of the period of these secondments (1968) that the original mission began to be challenged and the original courses programme was abandoned (1970); this is considered in more detail in Chapter 7 below.

Although the members of the teaching staff came from diverse backgrounds, their attitudes were quite similar in some very important respects. Virtually all of them showed a close interest in the students and gave them the respect they deserved as responsible adult learners; they were personally accessible and followed the pattern of intensive interaction with students established when the College was established. Many of them were younger than the students.

They were also competent. Former students agree that this was a critical factor both in their ability to learn quickly and in their subsequent attitude to further study. The College was fortunate in being able to attract staff who were not only committed to teaching mature students as effectively as possible, but were also of very high ability themselves. Their subsequent careers give some evidence of this. Three became heads of academic departments, two are senior administrators in international organisations, others either stayed in university teaching or moved into university administration. Several have substantial published work to their credit. This ability to attract high quality staff cannot be assumed in any future ventures of this kind. There is no doubt that for these young scholars,1960s east Africa seemed an exciting place to be. It proved almost as easy to recruit good staff as it was to recruit good students.

Experiences of the curriculum

The short course curriculum has already been described in Chapter 3, while that of the original long course appears in Chapter 4. With the development of an examined Certificate of Adult Studies, its curriculum content became rather more formalised and subject oriented, in line with the subjects to be examined for the Certificate. These were also some of the more likely subjects of choice for those who became undergraduates. Communication in English was central for all students: for the rest there was some choice from economics; sociology; political science; history and geography.

Essay assignments were a central tool of teaching and evaluation. Students on both the short and long courses were all stretched intellectually through these assignments. Marking schemes emphasised evidence of ability to analyse issues, ability to raise relevant points, ability to develop points raised, ability to present a well integrated discussion and to draw sound conclusions. It was this intensive tutorial process which most students saw as the most important part of the curriculum for them. Many referred to the small group tutorial and the one-to-one tutorial as having been particularly easy to learn from. They pointed out that the most outstanding beneficial aspect of these two methods was the face-to-face interaction and two way communication which permitted them to ask for clarification and to test out the validity of their own views. The learning group was like a mutual aid system in which students learned from one another with the guideline of the teacher.

When asked to describe the teaching methods they used at the College of Social Studies, the former teachers mentioned most frequently: small group lecturing; small group tutorials; one-to-one tutorials; written assignments; reading assignments and use of guest lecturers. Of all of these the small group tutorials and the one-to-one tutorials were assessed by the teachers as having been the most effective. Some teachers, however, did confess during the interviews that they were describing what they thought were the teaching methods they used, but they did not have a clear recollection of how they actually used those methods.

Nearly all of the teachers interviewed tended to view the curriculum of the college in terms of the individual subjects each had taught; only one or two of the 12 former teachers interviewed characterised the curriculum in broad, general terms. Otherwise it was seen as having been either to acquaint students with the economies of east Africa, the political issues of the day, or the implications of rapid social change for the culture, welfare and development of the students' societies.

A series of fortnightly guest lectures was also part of the curriculum. Guest lecturers were selected on the basis of their public position and their ability in given areas of interest to the current group of students. In particular, prominent politicians were invited to speak about national and regional issues of the day. Staff members who took an active interest in guest lectures rated them as having been a very useful element of the programme. Some staff and students described them as a useful substitute for field visits, while others viewed the lectures as having helped to reinforce ideas exchanged in the classroom. Some students found the guest lecturers inspirational enough to serve as role models.

Given the subsequent career success of former students, it is hardly surprising that their perceptions tend to be favourable. They all said they found the curriculum to have been pertinent to their lives at the time. Detailed memory of specific content was better than that of their teachers. For example, they said the courses threw into high relief such important issues of the day as whether or not a federal type of constitution was appropriate for Kenya; whether socialism or capitalism was the right kind of economic system for the country, and whether or not there were opportunities for building a racially and ethnically integrated modern Kenya. They pointed out that although they had heard about these themes before, they had not been equipped to understand their significance until the college furnished them with the appropriate theoretical background and systems with which to classify and interpret events. Another important part of course content stressed by many of the former students was the 'faster reading' programme arranged at the Kenya Institute of Administration. It was claimed that this increased their ability to consume a far greater amount of written information than they had previously.

Learning resources

The physical environment, the architectural design and geographical location of the college were all seen by former students as providing an ideal environment for learning. The attractive architectural design of the college was conducive to the development of an extended family type of social interaction. The buildings accommodating the classrooms, offices, the library, students' study bedrooms, the kitchen and dining facilities were linked together to form a quadrangle, inside which was the arena of social and intellectual interaction amongst both staff and students. Staff lived in housing on the College campus; and this made it easy and natural for them to move in and out of College all day.

The design for a *residential* adult education facility was deliberate and carefully thought through. The founders had certainly been influenced by the idea that this would be a kind of Folk High School on the Danish pattern (one of the original Capricornists in Kenya had personal experience of this). And in Denmark, their extensive use in national regeneration and 'nation building' was certainly well known at the time. Moreover, the early attendance at a short course of Richard Hughes the architect (himself an active Capricornist), was used in his 1963 re-design and extension of the building to facilitate even better personal interaction.

The library was assessed by former students as having been adequate for most subjects, particularly the social sciences; and it was the first contact most of them had had with a carefully selected collection of suitable books. There was a very good reference section. The fact that the library was small meant it was readily accessible. Moreover, there was little pressure on the resources of books and journals that were available. Another welcome feature was the good selection of books and learning aids for English language, particularly the programmed self teaching book on *English 2000*. The latter was found to be quite invaluable for those who needed remedial language learning.

The students were a critical learning resource for one another. The kind of students that ended up at Kikuyu tended to be interested in debate and to admire brilliant intellectual contributions to a debate or discussion. In this way, the student body constituted an intellectually stimulating and supportive environment for its individual members.

Allied to this was the relatively intensive interaction among students and staff. The staff and students had meals together, came together in the quadrangle during the tea-breaks and listened to the same, small College radio to hear and share in the analysis of the news. The geographical isolation of the College (about 12 miles outside Nairobi) helped to encourage this social interaction. Staff were given positive encouragement to share meals with students as frequently as possible, in recognition of the importance of such shared experience in breaking down social barriers.

This was part of the conscious attempt to break the mould of what had so recently been a racially stratified society. It was the first Kenyan educational institution to pay more than lip service to 'integration', both in terms of who taught and studied there and, perhaps more importantly, in the personal social relations which were encouraged. When the University administration brought to an end the practice of shared meals and tea breaks ('free meals' and tea for staff were thought to be undesirable), an important part of the carefully nurtured collegiality was lost. It was by the end of the 1960s both a symbol of changing staff and University attitudes and a significant contributory factor in the demise of the College (see Chapter 7).

The social relationships at the college were perceived and characterised by all respondents as having been among their most invaluable educational experiences at Kikuyu. Although some students confessed to having occasionally felt rather uneasy in the company of teachers they saw as their intellectual and social superiors, all observed that the experience was conducive to learning. Some of the former students pointed out that they remembered more what they learnt from those interactions than from classroom teaching or books.

The following key features were frequently cited by staff: informality; mutual respect; teacher/student interaction that de-emphasised differences in official statuses but was based on friendship and trust; open sharing of even personal concerns by students with their teachers; mutual learning and sharing of meals. All of these elements tended to deepen the teacher/student relationships. Further, former staff viewed these characteristics as having been the main force behind whatever success that the college had achieved with its mature students.

In sum, the student/staff view of the programme is that it was well integrated with mutually re-enforcing elements. The curriculum was relevant to the needs of the learners, the staff were competent, while most of the students were highly self-motivated and were found by the teachers to be a pleasure to teach. Indeed, both the former teachers and students made the observation, though using different words, that every element of the Kikuyu experience had an unfathomable and long-term impact on their own lives: it was a turning point for all those involved.

Impact and reasons for success

The evaluative comments in this section come mainly from the thirty year-old memories of former students; these inevitably selective memories tend to stress the positive aspects of their experience and perhaps to downplay the negative. They should be set alongside the contemporary comments from 1965 which are recorded in the following section (mature age entrants as undergraduates).

Among the most important features cited by the former students as leading to a lasting and important impact on their lives were the following:

- access to higher learning;
- career advancement;
- acquisition of a critical and analytical mind;
- widening of horizons;
- discovery of personal talents;
- acquisition of an appropriate work ethic; and
- acquisition of self-confidence and enhanced self-esteem.

Figure 1 1961: Lord Dulverton opens the College with a mainly "European" audience

Figure 2 1963: students and staff share a coffee break

Amplification of some of the above student comments helps to clarify the specific successes of the historical 'Kikuyu experience'.

Within a deliberately short 'academic year', the College was able to transform the intellectual capacity of a large proportion of its students, many of whom had not completed secondary school, into persons who could pass a stiff mature age entry examination for the University of East Africa.

Passing these examinations – designed to test academic potential – required relatively advanced communication skills in English and some mathematical aptitude. The Kikuyu experience enabled participants to acquire these abilities and to go on to make a success of their university studies as well as subsequent career advancement. As outlined in the following Chapter many former students rose from essentially clerical jobs, or from primary school teaching, to become senior administrators or academics or industrial managers. The former students themselves credit the Kikuyu experience with this success, pointing out that the decision making skills, communication skills, personal integrity, and the work ethic they acquired, were all part of the seeds for success which were planted at that time.

A critical and analytical mind was said to derive from essay writing and literary appreciation, as well as the one-to-one tutorials scheduled for defending essays by students. Many of the former students acknowledged with much gratitude that they learned to separate political rhetoric from political reality through the many exercises they had at the college in literary appreciation and in the analysis of national and international events. A 1996 comment from a local education officer was that 'Kikuyu produced intellectuals in the making, students who could read fast with understanding, take accurate lecture notes and write papers'. Wiltshire's idea of 'rigorous intellectual training' seems to have borne fruit.

Regarding the widening of personal horizons, former students saw this as deriving from the exposure they received from such courses as economics, geography and political science, which portrayed the interdependence of communities, regions and nations of the world; history, which explained how the students' countries came to where they were; and sociology, which presented a comparative analysis of social institutions in east Africa, thereby introducing to the students the concept of cultural relativity and the relativity of 'normality' itself.

Acquisition of self-confidence and enhanced self-esteem by former students was attributed by them to the intellectual skills they acquired from the programme as well as to the respect that was accorded to them by their own teachers. The feedback given by teachers on student assignments was always carefully worded so as not deflate a student's ego, even where negative feedback had to be given.

With regard to our two main themes, namely, access to higher education for mature students without formal entry qualifications and civic education for active participation in public life, it is evident from the assessment of the beneficiaries themselves that the success of the programme was greater in the area of providing second chance access to higher learning. The former students made relatively few direct remarks regarding enhancement of their ability to take on civic responsibilities and, except for a small number of outstanding individuals, there is little evidence of any increased willingness to do so. The closest they come to acknowledging this benefit refers back to the 'double edged' impact referred to in Chapter 1, where personal intellectual development is seen as enhancing decision making and management skills, and hence indirectly enhancing social and economic progress – what was described in the 1960s as 'nation building'.

There is a close contemporary (1962) parallel with the impressions of mature students at Ruskin College in Oxford. As with the CSS, there is less emphasis on the citizenship aspects than policy makers would have wanted and more on giving the confidence to proceed on an upward career path.

> *In its social role the Ruskin course mainly strengthens the confidence of students in their ability to meet middle class and professional people on equal terms.*[1]

The same study also records a *decline* in voluntary activity among the occupationally mobile.

Did the programme meet the 'conditions for sustainability'? It did address a real need for the participants, it was in harmony with the mission of the providing agency at that time, it was tolerated by the government of the day (until 1968) and it secured sufficient funding from both home and abroad.

Further, it was organised, promoted and taught by staff with a clear understanding and acceptance of the official mission of the college and who had the requisite professional competence to perform the activities relevant to its accomplishment. Tutors all emphasised second chance access to higher learning and it is precisely in this area that the programme had its greatest impact on the participants.

As for attractiveness to participants, there were far more people seeking admission than there were places and facilities at the college to accommodate them. Special essay assignments had to be given to those who wished to be admitted to short courses and the quality of performance and degree of self-motivation exhibited during the short courses were used as criteria for selection of students for the long course. Demand exceeded supply.

The curriculum of the College was seen by the students and former staff as relevant to the needs and interests of all concerned. Most of the people who sought admission to the college were interested in achieving entry into Universities, which the programme also emphasised. The range of learning materials made available at the college was viewed by all students as having been adequate if not generous. For most of the participating students, the College library was the largest single collection of books they had ever seen in their lives. There were enough books on all the subjects taught, supplemented by a wide range of learning aids, including books on how to study on your own.

Finally, a major feature of the adult education programme at Kikuyu was that the teaching approach, selection of content, and the treatment of subjects was particularly sensitive to the educational background and capacities of the participants. Indeed, approaches, content, and level of treatment were continuously adjusted to suit the somewhat varying capacities of successive generation of students admitted to the college.

Mature entrants as undergraduates

Information about the performance of former students as undergraduates derives from research conducted in 1965. Current memories of former students are now less clear about the distinctions between the learning experience at the CSS and experience as undergraduates than are those of some former staff.

Between 1963 and 1965, 89 undergraduates were admitted to the University of East Africa under the mature age entrance scheme: a number which represents between four percent and five percent of the whole intake; the CSS long courses made a small contribution to this larger total. Analysis of the educational background and examination results of this first cohort of mature undergraduates (Fordham 1966) revealed the following:

- Although success in the final year examinations was little different from that of younger entrants with 'A' levels, there were greater problems in the first year of study for the mature age entrants (61% of all entrants passed their examination at the first attempt in all subjects, but only 50% of the mature entrants did so).
- There was little correlation between formal schooling (including 'O' levels and/or teacher training) and success as an undergraduate.

- A period of full-time study beyond school did correlate with an ability to pass the mature age entrance examination.

The relative lack of success *in the first year* for mature students could not be explained by educational background alone: nor did we know enough about family circumstances to be clear about what disadvantages stemmed from them. The one certain handicap indicated by preliminary discussions with both staff and students seemed to be lack of preparation as students. It was with this in mind that Paul Fordham in 1965 interviewed all the ex-CSS students then at Makerere University College. What had been done to prepare them adequately and what had been left undone?

Most were concerned with the pace and volume of work compared with their previous experience, especially with the volume of reading. Interestingly, this provides a contrast with the somewhat rosy memories of thirty years later which are recorded in the first part of this chapter.

> *. . . we have quite a lot more reading to do here than we had at the College of Social Studies . . . Every time a lecturer comes in here, he brings a long reading list which perhaps we have to cover within one week and then we have another longer one.*

There was, of course some misunderstanding there revealed about the way a book list should be used. And it was clear that undergraduates were not receiving the kind of guided reading they had come to expect at Kikuyu. However, it was equally clear they had not been helped by previous close tutorial supervision at the CSS to cope well with the more impersonal style of a larger university. As another student put it:

> *I do not think anyone can read all the books on the lists which are given to us. What is really important is for the students to choose which of these books to read, in other words to be able to select the correct material.*

In spite of the emphasis already made at the CSS on reading techniques and communication skills in English, the question of slow reading speeds and poor techniques of study cropped up again and again in this 1965 group interview. As Fred Kabuye (from the first long course) put it at the time:

> *There is one technical difference between a mature-age student and a man who has come straight from school who has been used to reading and concentrating and sorting out things to put in essays. The major drawback is how fast you read a particular book; how you pick up what is important for your essay and set it out. This is for us a very big handicap.*

The 1965 research also shows that while CSS staff had been worried about working students too hard, they should have been more concerned about how best to work them even harder. As one tutor put it:

> *. . . at some stage in our first long course we felt we were pushing so hard that some of you were becoming over-anxious and I can remember the staff*

> *deliberately planning that students on the next long course should have . . . less reading. Now it may be that however unpleasant it is for the students being pressed at our College . . . it might be a better preparation . . .*

And so it turned out to be. Students who had been on the second, more leisurely, course were much more frightened by the volume and pace of work than the others from the first or from later courses.

> *I saw from the outset we have quite a lot more reading to do here than we had at Kikuyu. I do think we wasted quite lot of good time . . . It is only now that I realise I did.*

One result of these 1965 discussions was a change in emphasis for future long courses. *Inter alia* the College:

- made more conscious preparation for the pace and style of undergraduate work;
- instituted the rapid reading course mentioned above;
- placed even greater emphasis on good English communication skills, including the appointment of a full-time English tutor;
- gave extra training in study techniques.

There was also the start of recognising differences between students who had had secondary schooling up to 'O' level and those who had not and giving them different tutorial attention. The latter needed more specific subject content than the former and were the most able to benefit from the more formal syllabuses for the Certificate of Adult Studies then being planned.

The last point led to some early thinking about the future pattern of access courses which might be developed: thinking which was never to be put into practice, except for an experimental eight week course in study skills. Staff thinking at the time was that improvement in study skills *per se* could be achieved in a much shorter time than the 30 week academic year of the long course. It was hoped that these shorter courses might be provided in evening classes or in regional centres; but they were never financed by governments already becoming convinced that mature students were only 'necessary' or affordable at a time of shortage of qualified school leavers. What was then suggested were two types of access course.

The first would be for those already accepted as undergraduates, but who needed better study skills. This would be designed to avoid more costly failures in the first year of undergraduate study. The second would be something like the long course then being offered, but with more emphasis on cultural enrichment and filling out of subject content which had been lacking in previous formal schooling.

Already in 1965 it was found necessary to advance the arguments in favour of sustaining a mature age entry scheme. The scheme was being attacked as 'unnecessary' to meet manpower needs, or because it would no longer work when the supply of mature age entrants 'dried up'. But this is to anticipate the demise of the College at the end of the decade, the reasons for which are outlined in Chapter 7. What was not then discernible was how the political climate would change and affect the sustainability of the College, not merely because mature students came to be seen as an unnecessary luxury, but because the kind of civil society implied by the curriculum came to be seen as potentially subversive.

Note

[1]Blumler 1962 : iv

Chapter 6

Career paths of the one-year course students

The analysis of career paths is based on complete or partial information on 104 of the total of 130 students listed in Table 5.1 of the last chapter. As noted there, most came with a background of primary or junior secondary education. About half were primary school teachers and about half were from a variety of clerical or junior administrative jobs.

Destinations

The end of career destinations are much more varied than the background and jobs from which the students came. The following table is compiled from the information given in the last chapter and that summarised at the end of the book (Appendix 3). It records the last two known full time occupations of those for whom we have records. Where the last two job categories are the same, the individual is counted only once. In a few cases there is double counting (e.g. one politician became so only after he retired from a lifetime of teaching: another, an MP, was defeated at a general election and went into public administration as chair of a quango). Thus the table can give only an indication of the range of destinations and an approximate indication of the numbers ending up in particular kinds of occupation.

Table 6.1: Final occupations of former students. N = 66

Occupation	Number
School Teaching and Teacher Training	19
Public Administration	16
University Teaching/Administration	14
Private Sector Management/Administration	9
Private Business/Farming	4
Social Work/Community Development	6
Politics	4
Journalism	3
Law	4
Librarianship	3
Priest	1

This balance of occupations reflects the opportunities available throughout the 1960s, with the most rapid Africanisation in the early years in the public sector and, in the later years, in the private sector. What is outstanding is the range of senior and highly responsible positions to which many of the students rose. The selected personal stories which appear below, illustrate the range of career paths to the destinations recorded above.

Selected personal stories

Silas Ita

It was a turning point in my life. First, it gave me an opportunity to go university – an opportunity which would not have been there if I hadn't gone to Kikuyu. The other options for going to university were quite remote – and not as intensive in terms of preparation as Kikuyu was. Second, it exposed me to the idea that even adults can learn – intensively! Third, it opened up my mind to whole world of literacy. So it gave me a taste for reading further – looking for knowledge. And it prepared me for university work. It really was a turning point. It got me into a new kind of world altogether.

Before I went to Kikuyu I was a Chief. A Chief in the location. What has actually stunned people is how a Chief came to Kikuyu, and then went to university, and from there he sprung to various positions of responsibility, and he has contributed quite widely to the development of industry in this country! People don't believe it. They don't believe it! But it all goes back to that one year at Kikuyu.

That year, and the time at university which followed, gave me an opportunity to synthesise what I had been doing in practical life. It may be all written up in books – but I had actually gone through it in practice.

I was a teacher – I had taught for ten years. So I was able to link back to that experience when I was doing my Bachelor of Education degree. I was a Chief, and some of the work I had done as a Chief I found it in my studies of administration at the university. I was a Councillor – and we were reading about the local authorities in our university studies. So my work experience was a great help to me when I was a student at Kikuyu and at the university. I was able to place those practical experiences within a theoretical framework . . . to see how the two fitted together. It was very, very interesting. My time as a Chief was also a major experience – a package about tradition and culture that you would never get at university. And there are only a few sparks of it written up in various books here and there. But I got the totality of it. Perhaps I should sit down and write about those experiences. Now I can write about it. I can see it in both theoretical and practical terms.

I was not even married when they picked me as a Chief. But it was done through an election. Chiefs were being elected at that time. Having been a Councillor and a teacher, I was very popular in my location. So when we applied, and we were selected for interview and paraded for the people, and names were called – I scored about six hundred people behind me. And I became a Chief!

I went to Nairobi University. And I also went back for a Masters at the University. That is how I moved from Education to Business. CIDA gave me a scholarship to do the Masters programme. After which I was employed directly by the private sector. That was the Kenya Association of Manufacturers.

Then Government asked me to join the public sector – to come and revive the Investment Promotion Centre. They had tried two other civil servants to run the institution, but since IPC was private sector oriented, dealing with private investors, they needed someone who had private sector experience – and someone who understood private sector concerns.

I agreed. So they appointed me as Managing Director of the Investment Promotion Centre – where I worked from 1989 to 1991. Till the October of that year, when they established this new institution – the Export Processing Zone Authority. And again they found that they needed me here to come and establish this programme. That is what I have been doing for the last four years now.

Lawrence Mungai

I went to Kikuyu way back in 1964 for a three weeks programme. I was very young. In fact, I was from the University of Nairobi, where I was working as a clerk. But this was the first time that I felt the true university atmosphere. I became very interested in what was happening at the College of Social Studies, and I made enquiries about how I could go for the one year course.

One of the teachers at the University encourage me to take extra-mural classes. But I was a little disappointed with them, because they didn't lead to any kind of certification. But my real chance came. I wasn't very sure of myself, but I had the consolation that, even if I didn't make it to the University of Nairobi, I would get my Certificate of Adult Studies, which at that time was recognised as the equivalent of 'A' level. I decided to take four subjects rather than the usual three. At the end of the course, I didn't pass the mature age examination, but I did manage to get the certificate. But I was really disappointed, because most of my colleagues had got into the university. I didn't give up, though, and I passed the next year and proceeded to Dar es Salaam where I read Law.

Years later, I was seconded by the Government to Moi University, which was just being established. I was able to translate into reality the recommendations of the Presidential Working Party for the new university. It was the biggest challenge of my working life. But I cast my mind back and remembered how I went to Kikuyu and how we were not very sure that we would make it to the degree course, with all the competition. I still believe that the challenges I faced in my one year stay at Kikuyu are the primary source of the confidence that I have had in my working life.

Another challenge came when I left university – because I left prematurely. I got lost for some time, because I lost direction and perhaps even hope. But I realised I could still practise law – if I went to the School of Law. But here I was

– a very senior person, and they didn't have extra-mural classes and the Principal wouldn't exempt me. I had to go for a whole year. At one time I discussed the situation with my family, and I said: "I can't go to study with people who are my children's age". But my son said: "Look, you have to do something – why can't you go?" So I went to the School of Law because of the challenge of my son.

When I look round the table at this reunion, and see the kind of people who went through the Kikuyu programme, I can only wonder at the tremendous loss of talent – the tremendous loss of opportunity.

Patrick Muzaale

I left school at the age of nineteen, but I had gone to school at the age of ten. Which was quite early for our people then. I looked really too young to go to school. I was very tiny at the age of ten. So I left school early because my home was poor; the marriage of my parents was unstable, and they sometimes lived separately. However my parents contributed to my opportunity, and of course the native ability that I have was handed over to me by them! There was also my father's exposure in the King's court*. He came back determined to educate me and he gave me all these stories to show the value of education. So very early in my life the motivation to education was very, very high indeed. And I was promised a lot of things if I went to school.

Uganda then had a very complicated education system: There were four years in Lower Primary. Then you sat a very difficult public examination – to leave Primary 4 to go to Primary 5. Very few people made it. In my year there were forty-four of us who tried, and only three passed.

There were two years in Upper Primary. To leave Primary 6 was a great event – after another public exam country-wide. Junior Secondary was three years – and another public examination. Then Senior Secondary – and, of course, another public examination.

I dropped out at Junior Secondary level. I could hardly perform; being thrown out to look for school fees; going back; thrown out for one week – and so on. So I had to terminate my education in the ninth year at the age of nineteen. The lack of opportunities, and the number of hurdles to jump, came about because the country used severe rationing methods. These exams were intended as rationing – rationing the limited opportunities available.

I was fortunate to go to one of the best secondary schools, even though I had to drop out. But the teachers tended to favour those who were well turned out. The feed back I got was like looking into a distorting mirror.

I entered the East African Railways and Harbours Administration. The entry was highly competitive from Kenya, Tanzania and Uganda. I remember there were a thousand of us – and they wanted sixteen. I was fortunate to be amongst them. I did my clerical course, and was then posted to Nairobi as a railway clerk, where I worked for one year and then went for training as a guard –

*His father worked as an official in the court of the Kyabazinga of Busoga, the ruler of a small but progressive land in the south-east of Uganda where I came out as the best student of the year. For the first time I was photographed by newspaper people. I couldn't believe it! But that was when I was given my first positive feedback from the system. I was beginning to realise something about my native abilities. My work situation helped me to rediscover my abilities. And it brought me to Nairobi where adult education opportunities were more plentiful.

Being a guard was like being in the military. It was very tough. You had to take care of your train for 300 miles from Nairobi to Mombasa, and most of the journey goes though a National Game Park. Occasionally, the train would divide into two at night, and the regulations had it that you had to walk half a mile from your train to protect it, place a detonator on the lines, come back and wait for assistance. But you can imagine what it was like with roaring lions at night – and you are supposed to get out and protect your train.

On one occasion thieves came to my train and were picking out the big lambs from the sheep destined for Australia. I was forced to chase these thieves. When somebody warns you that thieves are throwing sheep from your train you have to do something! So I applied the brakes and the train stopped. I sent someone to tell the driver what had happened, and then I started chasing the sheep one by one, putting them on my back and throwing them in my coach. I'll never forget that event. What it did to me was to tell me that this was not going to be my lifetime's job. I had to do something else. A guard's job was a dead end job; there was nothing you could be promoted to.

The job entitled me to a house ten feet by ten feet. The good thing about that little house was that the railway welfare department placed a loudspeaker in it, connected to a very powerful radio which received the BBC from time to time. I would get my paper and pencil and listen to that golden English. Very keenly, I would write down some interesting sentences as they were thrown up. Some programmes were actually on the English language for foreigners and I was listening carefully, getting the words (I didn't know how to spell them often), getting down whole sentences, noting the English structure. So I used the radio time to educate myself in the English language. At the end of the programme I would get out my dictionary. It was a very poor dictionary, defining 'girl' as 'not boy', for example! But it is what I used. I started teaching myself. I would clutch at any piece of paper with some English words on it. And I had always a notebook to copy out any English sentence. I went on borrowing books from friends. And if you came to my caboose you would find a pile of books – all of them borrowed, none of them mine.

One day a stationmaster came to my coach and said. 'Patrick, you are not like other train guards. Whenever I come to your coach you are always reading and you have this pile of books, and you are always reading. What is going on? Are you doing a private course?' I said, 'No, it's just for the enjoyment of it.' He said, 'Really, can someone torture himself with books without any reward at the end?' He said, 'Have you ever heard of this college at Kikuyu, the College of Social Studies? You are the kind of person they would take.' He gave me the address and I wrote immediately and Paul Fordham immediately replied. He sent a questionnaire about my background, and I had to write an essay of 1,000 words, about either the economic or social or political problems of my country. I chose to write on economic problems. Apparently I was successful in my writing because I was invited not to their usual three weeks course but to a one week competitive examination course – apparently a pilot exercise.

Afterwards, and back home, I was afraid what the next letter from Paul Fordham would say. Eventually it came. I was afraid to open it myself. At first, I asked my friends to read it, and show by their faces whether it was positive or negative. However, I decided finally to open it. It said, 'I am writing with reference to your application for admission to the One-Year course and I am pleased . . .' Just to see the word 'pleased' I jumped. I didn't read the rest and went running around my house and people thought I was mad.

The letter invited me to the One-Year Course, and it said I would get a nominal payment for my family, and that the course was going to be supported from some Foundation. I went immediately to ask for permission to leave. The Railway agreed to give me one year's leave without pay. And so I left to join the Kikuyu College of Social Studies for one year.

But on getting there we were told nine of us had been admitted but there were funds for only eight and that one of us would have to drop off. Now this was something worrisome for me. I enquired about my friends' education, one by one. I discovered that I was the only person with only nine years of education. The rest had school certificates, and had taken an extra two years of education or training. In fact, one of them had gone to Makerere for a Diploma in Fine Art. So I knew I must be the one to drop off! When the results had been tabulated at the end of the first term I came second to the one with the Fine Art Diploma – and it was at that point that my confidence came back. I really felt that I was more able than I had previously known.

It was from there that I moved. I went to Makerere, after passing the mature age entry exam. I did not pass it as well as I had wanted. I went to do a Diploma, which I did very well – got a first class, and I was promoted to the second year of a BA course in economics, which I did very well. I got an Upper Second. And this opened the way to the rest of the world.

As soon as I got my degree, the National Bank gave me a job as a banking officer in training. After one month, I heard my name on the radio – the Uganda Government had appointed me as a government economist. Then I had an offer from the Department of Social Work, offering me a lectureship, because of my first class Diploma and my upper second. I went in as a counterpart lecturer and was sent to Manchester for one year. I also had an offer from the Faculty of Commerce as an Assistant Lecturer, and also from Economics. I didn't know how to make the choice. As a married person with children I didn't want to take any more risks – and so I accepted the full lectureship.

In Manchester, I did my Post Graduate Diploma. On my return, I was sent after five years to do my Masters and my PhD. In the US, when I was doing my viva for the PhD, I was asked a very unexpected question. I was ready for questions on my thesis, but this one was completely out. The Chairman of the

Committee said, 'Patrick, we are wondering how an intelligent person like yourself can decide to do social work. And you choose to do it in the US, where nothing at all resembles Uganda in any way. Why do you waste your time like that and spend five years in the States?' I was taken unawares and I had momentarily to pray to God for help. 'How do I answer, and still impress these people that I deserve to be given this degree?'

So I thought quickly and said, 'Let me tell you how I first came to know about this University. It was through the books that I read in economics. They were very highly rated books written at Berkeley. So I said that this must be the place where I must go – a place endowed with people of great talent and great analytical skills. I didn't come here to study social work; I came here to learn how to think. And I must say I am happy that my objective has been accomplished with this thesis.'

Later on, I was told I passed the viva with distinction.

From there, I became a senior lecturer. Most of my articles have been on nutritional deprivation and rural development – with a special emphasis on community based social work interventions.

Justus Mwathi

Before I went to Kikuyu in 1966 I had worked in various places. In 1954 I was a teacher. It was a very trying time. It was the height of the Mau Mau struggle, and only three months after I started work, my father was detained and I was left in charge of a family of some sisters, a brother and my mother. We had to move from the *shamba** to the 'emergency village', and anybody who belonged to a family of someone who was detained was not looked on kindly.

In 1962 I left teaching and moved to Nairobi and got employment with the Nairobi City Council as a clerk in the finance department. I didn't like the job, and the major reason was that my immediate boss was not very friendly. And then I saw an advert for a three weeks course at Kikuyu. . .

Kikuyu was very interesting, and it opened up wide horizons for many of us. And besides the studies, I quite enjoyed the confidence the students gave me. They elected me their president, and I played quite a role in student affairs. Eventually, when I went to Makerere for the Diploma in Social Work and Social Administration, I was still involved. The Kenya Government decided to discontinue married students' allowances, and we put up quite a battle. The Kenya students who had families there asked me to carry on, and finally we succeeded. One of the people who helped was Mr Nyagah who was then the Minister of Education.

I came to Kenyatta University in 1978, which is where I am now as an administrator. Where I will go next I don't know. But what I do know is that I am psychologically set to start another life. Because I don't like this idea of retiring. I don't like the word itself – it has such negative connotations. It sounds as though one is going to rest and wait to die. So I am ready for another change.

*Plot of land, sometimes quite small, and usually cultivated for subsistence food crops

Luke Odhiambo

I was brought up in a seminary, all the while from Standard Five until I left formal education. Father Gregory wrote letters to all of us at the end of Form Two, saying 'You don't have a positive attitude to being in the seminary'. We were not told why. I asked if I had made any mistakes. He said, 'No – but you must go to a teacher training college'.

I went home, and I met a cousin of mine who suggested that we should go to Mombasa, where he was working in cargo. "It is better than nothing," he said. When I reached there I wrote to my father asking him for some money, so that I could enrol with the Rapid Results College, the correspondence college in London. He sent me the money and I started studying.

Less than a year later I answered an advertisement recruiting people for secretarial training who would take over from all the Asians and Whites. When I went for the orals, they told me that I should take a one year course because I had done best in the English paper and yet I didn't have a school certificate. But I said that I couldn't do that because there was no working man in my family, and I needed a job so that the other children could go to school. So they agreed.

At the end of my secretarial course, I joined the Ministry of Information – as a copy typist. And I studied for my school certificate by correspondence. After Kikuyu I was supposed to go to Makerere. But because the university was breaking I didn't go. And the next year my name was missing from the list. So I applied to the *Agence France Presse*.

> I said, 'I want a job.'
> They asked, 'Do you know anything about journalism?'
> I said, 'Yes, I have been a journalist before.'
> I was given some work to do, and they said, 'You know the job.'

So I have been working for the *Agence France Presse* ever since. I like the challenge of it. I never gave up. I didn't throw my hands in the air and give up because I didn't go on to the university. I have been working normally. I think that is what we were supposed to have learnt as adults at Kikuyu.

Analysis of career paths

The teachers

With one exception, Andrew Olewe, all the teachers/teacher trainers started life in the teaching profession; and the one who did not 'imagined becoming a teacher' (he started in banking). Olewe saw the CSS as helping him 'to become a better professional'. His voluntary work consisted of trade union activities in the Kenya National Union of Teachers, of which he became a member of the Executive.

The career of Joram Ayoo is typical. A primary teacher when he came to Kikuyu, he struggled to secure a Cambridge School Certificate by private study (correspondence) and also attended extra-mural classes before going to the CSS.

He took a BA and Diploma in Education at the University of Nairobi and remained a secondary teacher (finishing with nine years as 'Senior Headmaster') throughout. He started, but did not complete, a Master's degree.

Some teachers either failed to proceed beyond the CAS qualification or took later sub-degree up-grading qualifications. This did not necessarily mean relative failure within the profession and several non-graduate ex-students made notable contributions to professional and public life, especially if they were associated with church or other community groups. Such teachers argue that the CSS helped to point them in the direction of civic activities.

Tobias Ayoki was already a fully qualified primary teacher when he came to Kikuyu and active in the co-operative movement; this had taken him to Sweden for short course training in this field. Active also in extra-mural classes, he then came to Kikuyu for both short and long courses. He subsequently had a long career in teacher education and as headteacher and, after retirement, became manager of a commercial organisation in his home area. He is also Vice Chair of a co-operative society, a leader of his church and a 'land elder'. He views the CAS as 'much higher' than 'A' levels. The Kikuyu experience gave him an understanding of people and skills in the management of social institutions. 'Throughout his working career he tried to treat his teachers and students like adults. He feels he has a broader view of life than his colleagues whose experience is limited to the formal school system. He said that many graduate teachers were 'immature and needed the kind of experience which Kikuyu alone seemed to give'.

Hezekiah Mwingisi Kisia was 'already reading privately' when he came to Kikuyu. He is one of those who saw the CSS course as his main motivation to proceed to further studies and who saw the course as 'better than university'. Now retired to the family farm, he is writing about his own local community.

The public servants

With some notable exceptions, most of the people in this category stayed in the same career line in which they started. Thus Henry Gachunga, starting as a health assistant became a Solid Waste Manager. John Njoroge, now a Deputy Secretary, came to the ASC as a clerical officer having completed Cambridge School Certificate. For this student and several others in the same category, the College was strictly a second chance route to a University with 'A' level entry requirements. Many claimed it was 'better' than 'A' levels because of the breadth of experience and curriculum to which they were exposed (see previous paragraph and under *Politicians* below). John Njoroge himself took a political science/public administration degree at Makerere and proceeded from there to a job in the District administration (as a District Officer). From then on his progress through the civil service hierarchy was steady and sure.

Some teachers also became senior civil servants via educational administration. Peter Sande-Jowi started life as a clerk in local government and rose to become Deputy Director of Education after a long career in both teaching and educational administration. He too speaks of the broadening effect of the Kikuyu experience and the quality of teaching he claims to have passed on to the 'A' level students he taught in school. He moved into administration through an interest in management and became one of the founder tutors of the Kenya Staff Institute. Stephen Oloo, also a Deputy Director of Education, remained on the one-year course for only part of the programme as he had entered the 'A' level examination as a private candidate and was successful. However his subsequent career in Education as an Inspector, and later as Education Attaché in London, he attributes to the quality of English teaching and the broadening experience of the Kikuyu course.

However, there were others for whom public administration was the chosen career after graduation rather than before. Two former railway workers illustrate the dramatic change in personal development and career possibilities which the CSS programme could offer.

Apollo Oluoch was an Assistant Stationmaster, and Paul Fordham remembers quite vividly the problems he had with academic work. His understanding and ability to learn were excellent, and it was on the basis of these capacities that he was selected for the long course. But he had no experience in writing academic papers and, had it not been for the remedial English programme and close tutorial supervision he would probably not have seen such later success. As it was, he went on to a post-graduate Diploma in Librarianship in the UK and rose within the Kenya Government service to become Director of the National Library Service. On retirement, he returned to the family farm to grow sugar cane and raise cattle.

Another Assistant Stationmaster, James Kigge, who became Cabinet Secretary in Uganda, had one of the most fascinating careers of all former students, partly as a result of the political upheavals in that country, his arrests and period on death row on trumped up charges (We have suggested he should write his memoirs, perhaps as 'A Civil Servant in Uncivil Times'). In retirement he chairs the Land Resettlement Task Force and the Police Tender Board. In conversation he recorded with vivid imagery his sense of wonder when he was suddenly transported to the environment of the College. How he valued being in the presence of so many books and of knowledgeable academics. Some of the staff had even written some of the books he read: 'it was as if I suddenly been presented with a Mercedes' instead of the inferior transport he had been using. At the same time he confessed to being a bit worried about having to go on talking to all the lecturers at meal times!

Kigge dropped out of secondary school because, as he suggests, he was at that time too lively to be well enough behaved. He went to Kenya to work with the East African Railways and progressed to Assistant Stationmaster before his 'brother', Patrick Muzaale advised him to go to the CSS. After graduating in English he could have become an academic, but he had 'already tasted enough of books' and wanted more action, perhaps in the police or the army. Instead he entered the civil service and eventually became its Acting Head. His brush with the army was in military prison rather than as a regular. This is not the place to record his descriptions of the cruelty of that regime, but his account of daily prayers by prisoners on the steps leading to the scaffold and his wry comment on the 'opportunity' given by nightly deaths from overcrowding (to carry out the bodies in the morning) give a flavour of what he endured with rare humour and personal integrity.

Academics and university administrators

Most of those in this category went into administration rather than teaching, and three became academics and academic organisers for the University of Nairobi in the Institute of Adult Studies. One of these, Joseph Mwaniki, has helped the authors in tracing other former students and has worked at the ASC as an Assistant Registrar. But the most distinctive professional contributions have been made by four former students who went into university teaching, two of them in adult education.

YMK Gwayambadde was already 39 years old when he came to Kikuyu, a primary school teacher and very active in several voluntary organisations and local politics. He was Head of Clans in Buganda, Secretary of a co-operative society and had also been a County Councillor. But his extensive experience was geographically and culturally very limited, and his command of the English language, especially in writing, was constrained by the vocabulary and sentence structure of the primary school. He blossomed at Kikuyu, and his mercurial personality made him an instant star when the College presented a live and topical discussion programme on Kenya television. However, his written English was probably the weakness which let him down and led to failure in the mature age entrance examination.

However, in 1962 it was still comparatively easy to find overseas scholarships. We still had faith in him and so did Ruskin College, Oxford where he proceeded directly. He never looked back. Having secured a first Diploma at Ruskin he was then asked to stay on and pursue a second in anthropology under Dr. John Beattie. This qualified him for award of a B.Litt (equivalent to a Master's degree in other universities), and with this he returned to Makerere as lecturer in social work. He stayed there until his 'retirement' to the priesthood and remained active to the end in various local community activities in Buganda.

John Okach was sponsored by his employer onto one of the first short courses in 1961. He was a trade union official and, at the time, a clerical worker. He was one of those recorded by the first Principal as in his view capable of a good honours degree at any UK university. And he was, of course selected for the one year course. He took to academic work immediately and, while the course at Kikuyu extended him, he became bored very easily when he became an undergraduate and did not quite live up to his early brilliant promise. However, he took a Masters' degree in the UK and became a tutor/lecturer at the Adult Studies Centre at Kikuyu. He played a key part in the events of 1969, which are considered in Chapter 7.

Thabo Raphoto was a refugee from South Africa and sponsored from the refugee school then being run by the African-American Institute in Dar es Salaam. Later he went to the UK on a UN scholarship to take 'A' levels and entered the University of Nairobi for his undergraduate studies. He is the only ex-student to become a university teacher in the field of adult education, taking a PhD degree at the University of Syracuse, where he later taught. In 1995 he returned to South Africa to work as Deputy Director of an Adult Literacy programme.

Patrick Muzaale (see personal story above) is another of the railway worker success stories. He left school after nine years 'because the home situation was poor; the marriage of my parents was unstable, and they sometimes lived separately'. After a period in the service of the EA Railways he realised that 'a guard's job is dead end job', there is nothing you can be promoted to. And he had already become a reader and had begun to amass a small library which he displayed in his caboose. After Kikuyu, a first degree at Makerere, a Masters' from the UK and a PhD from the University of California, he eventually became Head of the Department of Social Work and Social Administration at Makerere University. His work as an external examiner at another African university renewed his contact with Paul Fordham and led directly to his co-authorship of this book.

Private sector managers and businessmen

Until very recently, Kenya has provided more private sector opportunities than have neighbouring countries. Some former students found that these opportunities were so compelling that they turned down the offers they had to go on undergraduate courses and went straight into business. One, Joseph Mugweru, went straight into publishing and became an editor with a multi-national company; he now owns a bookshop in Nairobi, though he still claims a sense of inferiority because most of his drinking companions are graduates and some are university lecturers. Another, John Mbai Rucha, was taken on as a management trainee and stayed with the company for 18 years, rising to Divisional General Manager until he left to start his own business. He records that:

> *I studied privately during the time I was at Metal Box. I was interested in all round management, so I did a bit of import/export, I did a bit of marketing . . . When I look back I think my comfort in management jobs with my peers, was because I was a reading manager: they were not. After all their degrees there was nothing to read. So whenever there was any problem I always had it at my finger tips . . . One year in Kikuyu prepared most of our people for further university education. But it also prepared people for self study. It gave one that sort of confidence that you can sit down with your books and study anything at any time . . . There is that something inside there. I think it all started at Kikuyu.*

Silas Ita (see personal story above) has had a distinguished career in management since arriving at Kikuyu with only a primary education and experience as a Chief; he is now Chairman of the Export Processing Zones Authority. He believes that his time at Kikuyu became a 'turning point', both as an individual and in terms of his professional development:

> *As an individual the period introduced me to a whole range of skills for networking: something that is not taught in any other educational institution. If anything, as a mature student, I learned to network and work through people. That was the greatest asset.*

John Ajwang-Odongo started and finished his career with Barclays Bank, leaving the position of cashier to further his education.

> *Somehow I felt there was something, I ought to improve my future even in Barclays by getting something more than the 'O' level I had.*

He complained that he was 'mishandled' by poor managers and he felt 'goaded . . . to be a little bit better than these guys . . . so I resigned. He felt intimidated when he attended the special entrance examination because he 'saw a whole compound flooded with Peugeots . . . it was all very competitive'. At Kikuyu he said he 'was given the English language' . . . at University he 'wrote a lot of poems and at least one was published somewhere in a paper in west Africa and the title was 'Nothing Seems Tamed'. After university he rejoined the Bank until retirement and he is now Secretary of the Kenya Bankers Association.

Fred Kabuye-Nakusambwa left his primary school after only three years and thus had the lowest level of formal education of those who entered the CSS long course. However, he had gained a Cambridge School Certificate by private study (including correspondence courses) before coming to Kikuyu and as a result of a long period of self education, some of it as a boy soldier (nursing orderly) in the King's African Rifles, with whom he had been to India. He was unusually active in a number of voluntary organisations, including Toc H and a local social club, for whom he ran educational classes using his own personal library. After Kikuyu he took a degree in economics and then became an economic analyst for Esso, becoming departmental manager for economic affairs for three years until political upheavals disrupted a career which was never to be resumed in that form. Esso pulled out of direct activities in Uganda because of a government takeover of 60% of assets. After that, job insecurity and the advent of the Amin regime led him back to the University, first as Assistant Warden and later as Warden of one of the largest Halls of Residence. His business acumen never left him. When he retired he was able to start a small farm and, now in his middle 60s, grows vanilla as a cash crop besides providing food crops for his family and for sale.

The politicians

The most senior of the politicians, Honorious Kedikilwe, was in August 1996 Chairman of the ruling party and Minister for Presidential Affairs and Public Administration in Botswana. Like the one South African student, he came from the refugee school in Tanzania and then secured a scholarship to go to the US for his university studies. Back in Botswana, he entered the civil service, rising to become Director of Personnel before entering politics. The other politicians have less even careers.

Timothy Mibei said he was very happy and also very lucky to have gone to Kikuyu, because as a former teacher, 'wider visions were developed':

> *Colleagues from different parts of the country and the methods which were used enabled me to see far. It was as if a brick was being roasted and then ready to be used in building a house. Soon after I was promoted to the next grade. I became an Advocate of the High Court. I was employed as a magistrate. Kikuyu gave me life to struggle on and on. Eleven years and I retired as Senior Resident Magistrate. Kikuyu confirmed that:*
>
> *'Heights by great men reached and kept were not attained by sudden flight, but they while their companions slept were toiling upward in the night.'*
>
> *After I retired, I returned to English, African History and African Socialism, applying what I had learned I stood for election as an MP and went through at the first attempt in 1988. I was appointed Assistant Minister for Labour. Kikuyu made me know what John Donne said:*
>
> *'No man is an island unto himself'.*
>
> *Horizons were opened to see that we were part of the universe and that we have contributions to make to world peace.*

He is now Chairman of the Advocates Complaints Commission, having lost his seat in Parliament in the 1992 elections.

Meshak Isiaho came to the CSS with a junior secondary education and experience as an Assistant Chief. Since coming to Kikuyu in 1963 and following that a year at Ruskin College, Oxford, he has had a remarkably varied and rich career of public service and voluntary activity in his home area. For 11 years he was Principal of a Farmers' Training Centre and for nine years after that a County Councillor. His most recent foray into politics was to stand in a by-election for election to Parliament (he stood for the opposition and was declared defeated). He said that Kikuyu was the beginning of a new life. He could express himself in English and acquired a better understanding of economics, politics and the development of east Africa. He was motivated to continue educating himself and recording local history and trends in the development of political leadership. He is proud of his personal library, which he confidently says is the biggest in his community. Much of his voluntary work stems from his membership of the Society of Friends (Quakers) such as his membership of school governing bodies. But his Fellowship of the International Biographical Association is no doubt a result of his continuing scholarly interests.

A journalist

We have already looked at several examples of individuals who chose to go straight into employment rather than enter university. Lawrence Odhiambo did that, but not so much from choice as from frustration of his attempts to gain an academic education of his choice (see personal story above). He went to try his luck in the port of Mombasa where his cousin was working. Here he started correspondence study and later became a copy typist in the Ministry of Information and worked for a time in the newsroom of the Voice of Kenya; here he met 'the guy who actually taught me to write news'. After the CSS he was frustrated by the refusal of the newly independent University of Nairobi to admit him for a degree course even though he had passed the Mature Age Entry examination (he alleges tribal prejudice).

> *This is when I applied to the French news agency (Agence France Presse). I said 'I want a job'. They said 'you do not know anything about journalism'. I said 'yes, I have been a journalist before'. I was given some work to do. Within a day or so I was told there is no probationary period, you know the job. I have been working for the AFP ever since.*

International comparisons

Both the analysis given above and the selection of personal stories, show that the access to higher education theme was far more important for students than that of the active citizenship envisaged by the founders. Any social impact made by the CSS came from its impact on the small number of individuals touched by the College. This individual impact was often profound and certainly long-lasting; but no claim can be made that the CSS led to a significant strengthening of a sense of public service or in enriching the idea of responsible citizenship.

We should not be surprised by this. The life stories that have been recorded are little different from the life stories that can be found in other places and at other times. And everywhere, similar discrepancies can be found between the aspirations of the educators and those of the learners.

When the compulsory school leaving age in the UK was raised from 15 to 16, there were several pieces of Government-sponsored research into how the extra year might best be used. Among other things, one of these looked at the ranking of various school objectives by pupils, parents, teachers and heads. Whereas teachers and heads gave greatest weight to personal development issues like character building, knowing the difference between right and wrong and behaving well, the pupils and their parents emphasised career prospects, careers advice and learning things of direct use in their future jobs.[1] The potential conflict between the more idealistic objectives of the teachers and the more instrumental objectives of pupils and parents can be used constructively, especially if the differences are widely understood and debated; this certainly happened with some of the curriculum development work which was promoted at the same time, like secondary geography where a broader curriculum was combined with a tightening of subject discipline. On the other hand, when educators and the publics to whom they are accountable fail to keep their aspirations in step, then whole systems may become dysfunctional, as happened to parts of the UK school system in the 1980s, where many critics began to believe that schools were not serving the best interests of the economy. There needs to be awareness of the potential for conflict in the different aspirations, but also a readiness for constructive engagement.

In adult education, nobody has had more idealistic aspirations than Paulo Freire. Education for him was either for 'liberation' or social 'transformation'; the alternative was simply to maintain an oppressive status quo. And yet a recent evaluation of the last literacy programme in which he was personally involved (Movimento de Alfabetizacao de Jovens e Adultos [MOVA] in Sao Paulo, Brazil) shows the same divergent aspirations of educators and learners. In a perceptive outline of the 'key lessons' learned in this project, Stromquist gives pride of place to 'the substantial disjunction that emerges between the objectives of those offering a literacy program and those coming to avail themselves of its services'. Writing from a feminist perspective, she records that:

> *The women who read, in fact, used literacy skills for further integration into dominant stereotypes of women. Most of the MOVA women did enhance their feelings of self esteem and autonomy . . . (but) these affective gains did not counter their role in family and marriage.*[2]

Blumler's 1962 study of former students of Ruskin College, Oxford reinforces the view that mature student aspirations are concerned above all with individual improvement within the world as they find it, rather than enhancing social or collective responsibility or seeking social or political transformation. That may become a secondary or later result of the education then acquired, but it was not of first concern to students at the time.

Like the CSS long course, the Ruskin experience was valued both because it enhanced occupational mobility and also because it strengthened intellectual and cultural aspirations,[3] giving students the tools with which to think more clearly and reason more systematically. This may be an argument for trying to preserve the style and the curriculum of the programme, but it has little to do with the wider social or political aspirations of teachers who may wish to make a contribution to social transformation through teaching.

This study of ex-Ruskin students concludes that the main functions of Ruskin at the time were

- mobility promoting;
- stressing more 'academic' values;
- and giving students more individual self-confidence.

The conjunction between these conclusions and those of the present study is close. A concluding comment by Blumler is that 'adult students derive from a long-term course the benefits they seek when they enter.'[4] He argues that their attitudes and values do not change. If this is so, then for the providing agency there is the problem of reconciling realism, freedom of choice and the retention of an ethos that upholds the idea of service. Some of the implications for this study of these conclusions from Ruskin are considered in later chapters.

Notes

[1]Schools Council 1968
[2]Stromquist 1997
[3]Blumler 1962 : 385
[4]Blumler 1962 : 685

Chapter 7

The demise of the College

In mid 1968, John Fox, a tutor at the Adult Studies Centre on secondment from Nottingham University, was drawn to play Philip Ndegwa in the "monthly mug" competition at Sigona Golf Club. Philip Ndegwa was then the Permanent Secretary in the Ministry of Economic Planning – Tom Mboya's Ministry. So the occasion promised to be an excellent opportunity to take up a matter of urgent concern to the Centre: the Government had just confirmed that there would be no bursaries for the long course students of 1969.

In the clubhouse after the match, John Fox steered the conversation to the Centre, to the support that Tom Mboya had always given it – and to the dire consequences of withdrawing the bursaries. The response was as definite as it was depressing: 'With so many children leaving school with A levels who can't find places at university,' he said, 'there is no way the Government is going to support mature students.'

Philip Ndegwa went on to express his own worries about the rapidly increasing gap between academically qualified applicants and employment opportunities. 'Look at me,' he said. 'I am already a Permanent Secretary, and I am only 33 years old. And there are many graduates of my age holding very senior positions. That's very good for us. But before very long there will be a queue of young fellows piling up behind us – and it will be a long time till my generation retires. What's going to happen to those youngsters in the queue?'

So the Government decision to stop bursaries – prompted, as the Philip Ndegwa story illustrates, by the concern over the increasing numbers of qualified school leavers and the decreasing number of job opportunities – was an important factor in the demise of the long course at the Adult Studies Centre. It relates to the fourth of the 'conditions for sustaining adult learning programmes': that a programme can survive only as long as it secures sufficient financial support.

The Ministry of Education's decision regarding bursaries was communicated in a Circular from the Permanent Secretary. It reveals a remarkably shallow appreciation both of the plight and the potential of mature students. The Mature Age Entry Scheme was purely a 'stop-gap' measure in this eyes of this particular administrator. He was not untypical of the time:

> *I would like to point out that the* whole question of mature age approach is now no longer applicable. *Indeed strictly speaking the mature age system*

> *pertains to the period whereby the University was virtually* empty *and it was decided to encourage older people to take up courses at the College of Social studies before entry into the University of East Africa. At the moment we are* not really short of young students . . ..

Eventually, a grant from the Dulverton Trust for setting up a language laboratory at Kikuyu was diverted to pay the bursaries of the 1969 long-course students. But this staved off the problem for only one year. The 1969 course was the last of the long courses.

The language laboratory story also serves to illustrate the low priority afforded to adult education by the officers of the University of Nairobi. Without any consultation with the Director of the Institute of Adult Studies, the Finance Officer tried to persuade the Dulverton Trust to allow the laboratory to be placed within the Faculty of Arts. This only came to light some years later when Paul Fordham had access to the Dulverton Trust's files in London.

There were, of course, a number of other factors that constrained and eventually killed off the long and short courses programme at Kikuyu. The post-mortem might best be carried out by considering those of the 'conditions for sustainability' that turned negative.

Did the programme meet a real need?

Most certainly it did – as far as the students were concerned. The description of the curriculum and the students' response to it that we have given in earlier chapters should be more than sufficient evidence.

There might well be different views of what were the priority needs at the time. Griff Cunningham, for example, who was Principal of Kivukoni, the counterpart institution in Dar es Salaam, argued in the early seventies that his own curriculum was more precisely and beneficially directed to meet the nation-building objectives that both adult colleges had set themselves at their beginnings. Kivukoni recruited only those who were called 'leaders' in different spheres – politicians, trade unionists, community development workers, head-teachers – and took them through a programme that taught the tenets of 'ujamaa' (the Tanzanian adaptation of socialism) and a programme which Griff Cunningham unashamedly called 'ideological reorientation'. He was quite critical of the Kikuyu recruitment for the mainstay long course, which he said was 'merely providing an opportunity for a few individuals to better themselves'.

However, during the sixties and seventies in Kenya there were many thousands of Kenyans who had not received the kind of education that could stretch their talents. These were the people who applied for the courses at Kikuyu. Moreover, even though there was a sudden upsurge of school leavers qualified for university places there was still a shortage of skilled manpower. Particularly, there was a shortage of people with management capacities in all spheres – the civil service, business and education. Also, despite the undeniable fact that a main concern of the students was to quality for a university place (or other kind of professional training) both the short and the long courses at Kikuyu were based on a 'situation-centred' curriculum that involved an analysis of social, economic and political issues that were current in east Africa.

So the long course did not stop because the need for it disappeared. But in the minds of the decision makers, there were other priority concerns. As for the short course programme, it was already in 1968 being suggested that 'short courses should be aimed primarily at local leadership such as teachers, trade unionists and community development workers, and our own part-time tutors'.

Did the programme harmonise with the mission of the providing agency?

Within the staff group at the Institute of Adult Studies in the late sixties there was the same division of opinion that had begun to fragment the founding university adult education departments in Britain.

The third Principal at the Adult Studies Centre, Leslie Stephens, had been Principal of Fircroft College in England. So he himself was well in tune with his predecessors from the University of Nottingham, who had promoted the same kind of socially-centred and second-chance university adult education programmes that had been developed in extra-mural departments and in colleges for trade unionists such as Fircroft. But Leslie Stephens, because of his wife's ill health, had to cut short his contract in Kenya from two years to one. Also, the centre of decision making had shifted to the Nairobi campus, since work at the Kikuyu campus was now only part of a wider Institute within the University.

Institute tutors from outside the Kikuyu campus began to question the role of the University in promoting a liberal studies programme at Kikuyu – or school examination courses in the extra mural centres, for that matter. As in Britain, the traditional role of the adult education department was called in question: because, it was said, other agencies had grown up that could better provide non-university level and second chance education, and because the university adult education department should provide something more appropriate for a university – such as the training of adult educators and continuing education of other professionals. Also, the positive impact of mature-age students seems to have been no longer recognised by some of the staff within the Institute of Adult Studies as well as by Ministry of Education officials or university administrators.

So the sense of mission of the University and its Institute of Adult Studies was changing and diverging – and what Kikuyu was about, with its liberal studies short courses and its second-chance long course, was no longer an understood or central concern. At the Kikuyu campus, the Correspondence Course Unit, started in 1968, became a cuckoo in the nest. The emphasis shifted to the writing and delivering of correspondence courses for the upgrading of primary school teachers. And the majority of staff who worked at the campus during the day were driving to outside homes in the evening. An unforeseen consequence of placing the Correspondence Course Unit at Kikuyu was the destruction of the collegiate atmosphere that the first staff groups had tried so hard to create.

Was the programme permitted or tolerated by the controlling authorities?

In January 1969, John Okach, one of the very first students and then a tutor at the Adult Studies Centre, was arrested. He was accused of possessing subversive literature. The police confiscated two of his text-books. They were commentaries on the writings of Mao Tse Tung – and the fact that John Okach was a political scientist seemed to make no difference.

In actual fact, the confiscated books were not published by the Chinese Foreign Language Press and thus were not on the proscribed list in Kenya. (But the Inspector of Police who had arrested John Okach would not listen to such niceties. And when he was asked whether he had a warrant to search the Adult Studies Centre, he replied: 'I do not need a warrant. I can go where I like. I can search where I like. I can arrest who I like. Are you saying I have done something wrong?') Worse, when John Okach was first brought before the magistrates, the police opposed bail on the grounds that he had been subversive in his teaching. The magistrates accepted sureties, but John Okach was suspended from all college duties awaiting the trial. Eventually, the charges were dropped. But the whole episode left a sour taste – particularly that one of the students was a police informer, who left the course as soon as John Okach was arrested.

This event happened in a broader context of censorship and restriction within the country. One of the long-course set books, *Animal Farm*, had taken on a significance that couldn't have been anticipated when it was first selected. Criticism of the Government was not tolerated. As Hilary N'gweno, a popular *Nation* columnist, said when he was giving a lecture at Kikuyu about this time: 'A country can claim to be developed only when it allows people to make fun of its politicians – we have a long way left to travel in that direction!'

Apart from such humour, the kind of serious debate on social and political issues that was envisaged by the founding adult educators – and which certainly did happen in the early years of the College – could not happen in an atmosphere of intimidation and fear. Open debate in the seminar room was replaced by careful gossip between trusted friends.

When, in 1968, it was suggested by Government that the Institute of Adult Studies should promote courses on Sessional Paper Number 10 on African Socialism, the official statement of political and economic policy, the invitation was politely turned down. The staff did not believe that they would be allowed to treat the document in an honest and critical manner. 'We are not into the business of propaganda,' one of them said.

Was the programme organised, promoted and taught by staff with a clear understanding and acceptance of the providing agency's mission – and with the required professional competence?

Above, we have argued that one of the problems facing the staff at Kikuyu who were committed to the liberal studies programme and the long course was that by 1968 a number of staff in other divisions of the Institute were beginning to suggest alternative programmes. Their problems were compounded by the fact that most of the recently appointed staff had not shared the experience of what we have called, in shorthand, the Nottingham tradition: problem-posing, discussion-based teaching.

By 1968, a number of staff had been recruited for whom their position at Kikuyu was more a job than a mission. They had had no previous teaching experience, and they were given no formal orientation. In his short period as Principal, Leslie Stephens did try to build a sense of team-work and purpose – but his time was unfortunately cut short. As Tom Mulusa recollects:

> *We were all working round Leslie. He wasn't driving us but he was stimulating us to think; and he was making us feel that we were doing something important. Perhaps, unconsciously, we wanted to show him that we could be as productive as he wanted us to be. And when he suddenly left, some of us were in a state of shock. For a time we didn't really have a sense of direction. And, with Leslie gone, those staff in the Institute who didn't believe in what we were doing at Kikuyu became more outspoken.*

And following Leslie Stephens' departure a number of staff were recruited – and given management responsibilities – who were quite young and untried.

'Some of the staff came in directly from university,' says Tom Mulusa. 'They had no field experience, and they were not given a professional training programme that might have compensated somewhat for their lack of experience.'

> *I remember sitting in a teaching session give by one of them. He was simply reading out some notes he had made when he was at university himself. When the students asked questions, he could only repeat what he had read. He had no other way of responding. The staff became younger and less experienced. There was certainly a decline in teaching standards.*

Not only that; but by the late sixties there was serious decline in commitment on the part of some staff. They had other kinds of commitment – outside interests. They seemed to regard Kikuyu as only a staging post on a career path that, they hoped, would lead them to greater public exposure and, of course, more pay. A few of them began to miss lectures, and pay too little attention to marking written work or holding tutorial sessions. One recruit to the teaching staff somehow managed to be paid for several months without conducting a single teaching session!

Staff and students lived more separate lives. The collegiate spirit evaporated.

Chapter 8

Learning and training for active citizenship

Education for citizenship: the case study experience

'Citizenship' is a slippery concept. It changes meaning from place to place, from time to time and according to the ideological positions of those who discuss it. The case study has shown how the idea of a College of Citizenship, dedicated to the development of a 'multi-racial' Kenya was quickly overtaken by events in the wider polity. Citizenship on the lines of Colonial Office white papers or the Capricorn Africa Society gave way to the idea of 'nation building', though in this case the character of the nation to be built was never clearly defined. In any case, the students at Kikuyu, like their contemporaries at Ruskin in Oxford, saw in the new college an opportunity for personal and career development which they seized with great enthusiasm; it was only on mature reflection that they came to see the programme as 'double edged', helping to make them into confident decision makers in whatever walk of life or level of employment they were in.

The original underlying purpose of education for citizenship within the liberal democratic state begged many important questions, like what kind of state was to evolve, whether the wider social purpose was reflected in the students' own motivation or whether such a programme could be sustained indefinitely. Until the late 1960s, the professional tradition of staff at Kikuyu still included some emphasis on the collective good and social justice in the educated society, while the individual learners were enabled to pursue their personal career goals and individual self fulfilment. But the case study does reveal a learned 'citizenship' element amongst former students, not in the sense of a stronger national identity or of state patriotism, but in the career choices made and the sense of responsibility many of the individuals recognised. An emphasis on public service and/or personal integrity in business affairs and a continuing belief in democratic participation in the face of a repressive polity seem to be hallmarks of this now middle aged or elderly group.

As long as a plural political system remained in place (until the late 1960s), the liberal democratic style of education practised by Wiltshire and his successors could survive unscathed, largely unchanged and only fleetingly challenged. Such challenge as there was came from socialist educators, like those at Kivukoni College in Tanzania, who thought that Kikuyu put far too much effort into the career development of a few talented individuals, and almost nothing into leadership training for nation building. In Tanzania this meant training for officials of the ruling party or the systematic induction of teachers and other influential groups into the values of African socialism as promoted by President Nyerere. For a brief moment in the 1960s there was a challenge in Kenya from a newly created and openly political 'Lumumba Institute'; this aimed to be more like Kivukoni. But plans for this new college soon fell victim to an increasingly intolerant political regime.

What kind of citizenship?

This chapter is written from the perspective of late 1990s Britain, where a decade and more of 'New Right' ideology, and its influence on the organs of state power, have all but eliminated the idea and value of learning for citizenship. Instead of an education concentrating on a newly enfranchised working class (or later, other categories excluded by gender or race), the redefinition of the citizen as user or consumer of services has emphasised a limited range of rights and a limited information system to support them. Citizens have been offered government sponsored 'Charters' to announce and be able to claim those rights; but it has been up to them as individuals to seek to exercise them. They did not need to learn about responsibility within an active citizenship. By 1997, the particular tradition of civic education from which the CSS sprang had been all but eliminated. However, in the late 1980s there were the beginnings of a new debate about the meaning of citizenship[1] and this debate has included new ideas about what education for citizenship might be needed: 'active citizenship' is once again part of educational discourse in a number of countries.

Within this discourse, attempts are being made both to re-define and to re-locate education for citizenship. For example, in Britain, renewed interest in citizenship has led both to increased activity by political pressure groups like Charter 88, pressing for constitutional change, as well as to educational research which has enquired into questions such as learning within social movements and the changing relationships between civil society and the state. And at the international level, the *Hamburg Declaration on Adult Learning* begins with the assertion that adult learning

> *is both a consequence of active citizenship and a condition for full participation in the life of society. It is a force . . . for fostering sustainable development, promoting democracy and justice, and building a world in which violent conflict and war are replaced by dialogue and a culture of peace.**

Recent writing about adult learning for citizenship has used TH Marshall's 1950 analysis, which divides the concept into its civil, political and social dimensions. The civil dimension refers to all those legal and other rights which are necessary to ensure personal freedom; the political dimension refers to equal rights for

*Adopted at the Fifth International Conference on Adult Education, July 1997, UNESCO

participation in democratic decision making, while social citizenship refers to welfare rights and basic security for all individuals. Citizenship 'expresses our inescapably dual identity as both individual and member of the whole, the public; our duality as autonomous persons who bear responsibilities in the public domain.'[2]

Now the liberal tradition in the UK (as did the variant exported to Kenya) tended to assume the existence of established and secure civil and social citizenship. What seemed important was to extend the political dimension to previously excluded groups. In the UK this was initially (in the 1920s) a newly enfranchised working class, while in east Africa it was the African majority. Capricorn saw the means to this extension of political rights as promotion of a 'multi-racial' polity, whereas the other founders were content to be a small part of the movement for greater civil, social and political rights for Africans. In each case, it was not the existence of civil or social citizenship which was questioned; all shared a belief that other individual and social rights would follow from the extension of political citizenship. The major question at the time was how this could or should be controlled and guided. Or was the extension of universal suffrage alone a sufficient condition for universal citizenship?

In the event, all of the initial assumptions were to be undermined. Citizenship in all its dimensions has proved a fragile concept in many newly independent countries, not least in Kenya. The institutions of civil society have had to work hard to survive the centralising and authoritarian tendencies of what Gertzel so aptly called the 'administrative state'.[3] State power remained centralised as under colonial rule and the state continued to be administered by the District Officers and District Commissioners whose offices were inherited from the colonial state. Democratic local government was allowed to atrophy or never really took off. In 1997, the President attacked the idea that constitutional and other political issues might be discussed by 'civic education seminars organised by non-governmental organisations'. He advised that NGOs should concentrate instead on raising living standards. This is not so far from the strong belief of many 'New Right' ideologues that education in all its forms should serve primarily the needs of the economy and, for the majority, be explicitly, even quite narrowly, vocational. The debate about liberal education is not about its value but about the people to whom it should be extended.

There is an attempt in the 1996 Delors Report to re-establish the idea of civic education as part of the practice of citizenship, and to do so in a way which has universal validity. Not only must each person 'learn how to learn' in a system of lifelong education, but learning to know, to do and to be should be accompanied 'by learning to live together'. For adults, this should support a

> *synergetic relationship between education and the practice of participatory democracy . . . to build an active civil society which, occupying the middle ground between scattered individuals and a distant political authority, would enable each person to shoulder his or her share of responsibility in the community, with a view to achieving true solidarity.*

The goal of civic education is defined as:

> *the ability to play an active part in envisioning the future of society*[4]

If these are desirable goals, then the question arises: in what contexts would they be both possible and sustainable if attempts were made to implement them?

Civic education in context

These contexts are both global and local. For the global, Johnston's commentary is apposite:

> *the world is changing: in economic terms, with the globalisation of capital and the pre-eminence of market considerations; in social terms, with the polarisation and fracturing of the labour market into a core/periphery/unemployed model, the increasing questioning of the welfare state and the emergence of a socially excluded underclass; in political terms, with the decline of the nation-state, the growth of international issues and interest groups and the problems of stateless people; in cultural terms, with a wider acknowledgement and assertion of cultural diversity and pluralism amidst a new global emphasis on consumption; and in terms of knowledge, with a questioning of the grand narratives of science, rationality and human betterment . . .* [5]

It should also be recalled that the UK liberal tradition was highly localised and relevant to its time and place of origin. In the form in which it was exported to Kikuyu, it might have been expected to fail even earlier than happened in fact. What has to be considered are the elements which sustained it in the short term, what might be relevant in the future and in what contexts.

In any local context, one crucial element in maintaining sustainability is the relationship between civil society and the state. When this relationship fractures, it is difficult to envisage any civic education being tolerated which is concerned with the political dimension. When the College was established, the major issues for public debate were constitutional (how much power to the regions?), social (how to achieve greater racial integration and equality?) and economic (what was the meaning of 'development' and how could it be achieved?) It was around these and related issues that a problem centred curriculum was created. Such a curriculum later came to be seen as unnecessary and potentially subversive; this was a major cause of the demise of the College and the situation in that local context seems little different in 1997. However, local contexts can change in a more favourable direction.

In countries where the idea of 'good governance' or existing constitutions are being looked at anew, the time has come for a fresh attempt at 'education for citizenship'. Proposals have been made which envisage citizenship colleges, like the one planned by Capricorn, along the lines of the original (nineteenth century) Danish Folk High Schools, themselves concerned with establishing a national democratic identity. Paul Fordham recalls he was in 1967 saying much the same thing in a public lecture in Kenya – that adult education should help build a common sense of belonging and sense of purpose in the new nation state.

However, the trouble with both these ideas is that, unlike the Folk High Schools, they do not derive from indigenous grass roots movements, but from ideas imported from other countries and cultures. A sense of belonging and of solidarity is obviously important for political growth and development, but it is unlikely to be created in response to programmes thought up from outside. In these circumstances it may be doubted whether any education *for* citizenship could succeed, especially if its opponents saw it as propaganda. One can envisage an adult education curriculum which helps civic consciousness and better informed public decision making; but this is quite different from trying to promote a pre-determined form of citizenship.

In one of his last interviews, Paulo Freire defined citizenship as 'the exercise of being oneself in the context of the state'[6]. While he went on to demand an accompanying political mobilisation which would certainly not be universally acceptable, his definition, *locally applied,* provides a useful starting point in any context for thinking about what kind of civic education is either possible or sustainable. Even if greater political or social action is the aim (and it may not be), this can only be accomplished by numerous individuals becoming aware of the possibilities for change and themselves determining to take action. It is debate at the level of groups who see themselves as communities or which have a sense of belonging which is now significant; but these local debates have also to be taken together with global concerns like environmental issues or unemployment.

Moreover, changing and overlapping global and local loyalties, do not always coincide either with state boundaries or with notions of the nation-state. The world is both global and local: changing and interdependent but also stubbornly fragmented. Independent Kenya never agreed a clear vision of its nationhood; and in 1990s Europe, global ideas and local loyalties alike either struggle for power and influence within the old state structures, as in the UK, or actively sought to overthrow them as in the former Soviet Union. In most of Africa, ethnic loyalties were never over-ridden by national ones and the idea of 'nation building' was more myth than reality. Perhaps only in the new South Africa is 'nation building' part of the current reality on that continent. In most countries we are all in the process of re-defining our overlapping loyalties.

Some newly independent countries like Tanzania did make the attempt to define the nature of the state and of civic responsibility within it; and adult education was pressed into service to help that process, as at the Tanzanian 'Ruskin' (Kivukoni College). But that was closely tied to an advocacy of 'socialism' and died in the failed attempt to create it. In Kenya the attempt never really started, and was quickly replaced by increasingly ethnic politics as existing language groups, and communities identified by that and/or culture and geography struggled for influence, power and access to land.

The conclusion must be that 'building an active civil society' may be a desirable goal; but that the means have to be defined in a multiplicity of local contexts. Similarly, there can be no education for citizenship without examining the range of purposes which heterogeneous groups of learners wish to pursue. However, that still leaves to be examined the *educational* legacy of a College where the original purpose of creating better and better informed citizens actually seems to have served to promote career development very effectively as well.

The liberal tradition: essential educational components

Up to this point we have looked at the 'Kikuyu experience' from the perspective of former students and teachers. We have also spoken of the transformation of intellectual capacity and of the rigorous and intensive intellectual training given through study of aspects of the social sciences; these Wiltshire argued were 'most appropriate to adults since they are the studies for which experience of affairs is at least as valuable a preparation as classroom study.'[7] It was also true that such a core curriculum gave rise to lively debate about all the contentious issues of the day and, inter alia, made a small contribution to civic education in that time and place. However, what concerns us here is whether the 'double edged' impact of the programme (which was also good at encouraging and bringing out the talents of mature age adult students) is worth re-creating for similar purposes in any context.

Perhaps the best summary of the values and methods behind the tradition is that offered by Fieldhouse.[8]

> *(it) implies a democratic, dialectical and non-utilitarian approach. It is democratic rather than authoritarian, with the students enjoying the right to choose what and how they study. The class is treated more as a mutual exploration of the subject than a one-way transmission of a body of knowledge from 'expert' lecturer to ignorant students. It is dialectical rather than propagandist, with a total freedom of discussion of all subjects. And it is non-utilitarian . . . in that it is concerned with the education of the individual for personal intellectual advancement or to make the individual a better educated citizen. This liberal education is thus concerned with developing the students' critical faculties and their ability to question all existing assumptions and to enable them to formulate, or at least understand, alternative interpretations. No issues or positions should be exempt from this rigorous and critical analysis. This process should open out and indeed challenge the students' conceptions of their own environment, widen their experience and understanding, and thereby increase their awareness of alternative conceptions.*

Additionally, it was argued that the liberal tradition offered *the intellectual tools to play a full role in a democratic society or to challenge the inequalities and injustices of society. . .*

Furthermore, Fieldhouse argues that content is less important than the method of teaching.

> *It is concerned with giving people access to the arguments and helping them to make up their own minds: it is a tentative, provisional and undogmatic approach:*

> *it is an openness of mind and a readiness to listen attentively to what other people are saying: it is the avoidance of preaching any specific attitudes or beliefs: it is the desire to develop students' powers of independent judgement. . .*

And, it is important to add, these values and methods can apply to any adult learners, not simply an existing elite. To think otherwise would imply a very narrow popular base to citizenship, however that might be defined.

The experience of mature students at Kikuyu, Ruskin and other adult colleges is that this kind of teaching is also a very good training for further progress in higher education, stretching the mind without preconceptions about what might eventually be the chosen course of study or subsequent career path. It is the elements of flexibility and openness which continue to impress, and which former students believe led to the development of critical and analytical minds, widened horizons, the discovery of personal talents and confidence in themselves.

There was of course an instrumental element in the curriculum, if only because of the deliberate concentration on techniques of study and communication skills. But for adult students, struggling to make sense of their own lives, the curriculum and style of teaching of the liberal tradition, which emphasised core skills rather than specific knowledge, made better sense and gave openings to a greater variety of opportunities than would have happened with a more narrowly devised access course already in thrall to the subject based approach of the local universities. Adult learners seeking entry to higher education do not always know what existing course will be most suitable for them until they have had experience of enhancing their understanding of personal experience through knowledge and skill training which extends from it.

Skill development for decision making

The argument that the Kikuyu experience of liberal education was 'double edged', stems from the perceived effectiveness of this kind of education for future managers, administrators and leaders in public life, including politicians. It gave confidence and enabled the discovery of personal talents hitherto not revealed. But it also gave skills which are like those needed by decision makers in all walks of life and which modern management training also seeks to instil.

The rigorous intellectual training offered by the College made it possible to:

- gain experience of acquiring and weighing the importance of evidence;
- develop the skills of rational debate and argument;
- recognise that almost all management and life decisions are based on whatever limited evidence is available;
- retain an open mind about whether decisions and opinions need to be modified in the light of new evidence which may become available;
- develop the capacity to challenge often cherished assumptions and beliefs about the environment from which the learners come and in which they live.

Openness, flexibility, personal confidence and an ability to listen to others, all of which should accompany these skills, as well as personal competence at the chosen profession or role, are the hall marks of the successful decision maker in any walk of life. Although there is no necessary connection with any direct education or training 'for citizenship', the effect on the individual is the same.

In making this assertion, we recognise that the methods and style of the adult learning we have been talking about, derive from those of undergraduate teaching at Oxford and Cambridge, where the tutorial system dominates and where there is no doubt about the intellectual challenge to the individual learner. The content of the curriculum may be different, deriving as it does from a range of topical adult concerns and existing experience and crossing traditional subject boundaries. But the essential tutorial basis is the same.

There are echoes of many of these issues in modern – or post-modern – discourses about adult education. That the participation of learners in programme development and management is desirable is now a commonplace notion. Programmes organised with close reference to the intended learners, are preferred to those simply thought up and tried out by administrators. The ideas of Paulo Freire and his followers have ensured that what is considered relevant knowledge has to be negotiated with the learners, rather than drawn exclusively from the existing or traditional 'bank' of knowledge in university or other libraries or from the minds of 'experts'. These are of course parallel discourses and do not stem directly from the liberal tradition; but many of the underlying values are the same, like a belief in the educability of ordinary people and in their capacity to undertake civic and other social or management responsibilities, even if they come from groups which currently suffer from social or political exclusion on grounds of class, race, ethnicity or gender. The politics of promoting civil society and an inclusive citizenship are central to current adult education discourses.

What may sometimes be left out of these discourses is the intellectual rigour which was central to the programme at Kikuyu. Now it has already been argued that the liberal tradition and its 'essential educational components' are part of the practice of the older UK universities, themselves even now the preserve of an elite or potential elite group. What happened in the UK was the transfer of an educational tradition designed originally for the few and its application to groups which it was intended to incorporate into a more inclusive citizenship. The concentration in the long course at Kikuyu on those considered exceptionally able intellectually, helped reinforce the view that the College was elitist and interested only in offering individual advancement to a few fortunate individuals. It also helped obscure the concern central to the open entry short courses that *all* students should have a short period of intensive intellectual training. Although this may seem a point of departure from modern discourses it also provides the direct link with them: a belief not only in the educability of ordinary people but also that intellectual rigour is an important component of any education for a more inclusive citizenship. In curriculum terms this is certainly a point of departure from those for whom relevance may be more important than rigour. It is our assertion that both are important.

Of course, there are many modern universities where other methods predominate and which do not use the methods described, and from which the students at Kikuyu derived so much benefit. Even in the 1950s Wiltshire was fond of asserting that Adult Education Departments were the 'last refuge' of the liberal studies. But for adult learners, who sometimes have to unlearn as well as to learn, and who will feel in a hurry to 'catch up', there is no substitute for an approach which tries as quickly as possible to develop the skills listed above.

If a similar College or programme were to be established in the future, the liberal tradition would need both to be re-invented and re-defined. For instance, the increased use and complexity of modern information technology, and the wider access to knowledge it can bring, would re-shape the curriculum and change methodology. But the essential pre-conditions for the development in confidence and ability of adult learners would remain the same. That is, that learning should take place in the context of open debate, where dialogue is preferred to preaching and education to propaganda. If we are to believe the evidence from the former CSS students, this is the way people gain access to higher education *and* become successful managers, both in their jobs, their local communities and in the wider world: good businessmen, professionals and administrators. And good citizens too.

Notes:

[1]Hall and Held 1989; Hooper, Farrell and Hedge 1995; Field (ed) 1991; Usher, Bryant and Johnston 1997
[2]Ranson 1994
[3]Gertzel 1970
[4]Delors 1996 : 22, 63, 61
[5]Usher *et al* 1997 : 28–29
[6]Stromquist 1997 : 217
[7]Wiltshire 1963 : 71
[8]Fieldhouse 1985 : 2–3

Chapter 9

Access, civic education and sustaining open learning

The purposes of adult learning

Part of the current professional discourse in adult education and training is to emphasise adult *learning*. There are several reasons for this. First, many educators of adults like agricultural extension workers or health aides are seldom part of the debates of those who see themselves as adult educators. Secondly, adult learning for specific purposes happens both inside and outside educational systems. A water development project which involves learning about pump maintenance and its management is certainly adult learning, but it may not be labelled adult education or even adult training. Thirdly, particularly in the English language tradition, the separation of the ideas of training on the one hand and of education on the other, has had a damaging and divisive effect on public policy making. Training for the enhancement of job-related skills, the core of 'human resources development' and currently in the ascendant, has been seen as different from, and perhaps in opposition to an adult education which has focussed more on personal development, empowerment of social movements or the support of civil society in general. The new focus on adult learning is part of an attempt to bring these two strands of thinking together.

Adults will be motivated to learn for purposes which they themselves feel part of and which they also help to define. If local issues and purposes for learning are both to reflect, challenge and change global concerns and action, then adult learning in different local contexts must reflect both the personal/social as well as the economic purposes for which programmes may be provided. Issues like unemployment, gender imbalances or environmental degradation not only cross the boundaries of the economic and social sectors of any economy, society or polity, they are also interwoven within the consciousness of individual learners. A 'double edged' curriculum like that offered at Kikuyu, could still offer access to more formal learning for the under qualified as well as serving the great variety of civic purposes, achievement of which brings about a more inclusive citizenship.

There may also be a practical reason for bringing the training and education visions together within a holistic concept of adult learning. Work with marginal or with socially/economically excluded groups like the unemployed, has shown that simply providing a vocational training curriculum may not work well, either in terms of motivation or of the intended effects. The question has to be asked in any society, who is currently seeking access to formal education?

For the UK, Jackson uses a 1989 survey in the city of Birmingham to argue that to define adult training solely in terms of human resources development for the labour market may be counterproductive.

> *. . . education is a form of human exchange, which, if it is to be effective, requires participants to be creative partners acting individually or collectively in different circumstances and according to the interests which lead them to look for relevant learning. If the aim is . . . to increase the skills base among adults for economic reasons, we have to take seriously evidence that people who do not take up formal vocational courses because they lack confidence or motivation, can begin learning through other kinds of activities and then move on to formal learning. These are activities they undertake as people, as citizens, as members of society, not commodities in the labour market.*[1]

In the east Africa of the 1960s there was a large pool of highly motivated but under qualified would be entrants to higher education who believed, quite rightly, that the Kikuyu courses would not only offer them access to higher education but also to well paid employment opportunities. We now live in a different era. Not merely do we have the 'interdependent but stubbornly fragmented' world noted in the previous chapter, but the labour market conditions are now also quite different. When the Kenya Government withdrew support from the long course at Kikuyu, one reason given was that it was no longer needed to meet estimated manpower requirements. Now, as in the Kenya of 1968, if any country wishes to include those now currently excluded from access to higher education, this will require arguments which go beyond immediate labour market requirements. Planning will have to take account not only of possible ultimate destinations in education or employment, but also the great range of motivations to learn which derive from local concerns. The phrase: 'think global, act local' has become something of a truism. To maximise opportunities for adult learning we may have to turn this on its head and talk instead of 'think local, act global'. Only in this way is the problem of social fragmentation likely to be addressed and a more inclusive citizenship assured. This is also the way to maximise opportunities for access to higher education.

Access and civic education

The nature of demand and provision for access to higher education is global: for civic education it is mainly local. Of course, such a sweeping statement must immediately be qualified. The demand for better access comes from two directions: either from employers and the state authorities, who see extending access as one means of increasing economic efficiency; or it may come from individuals who are already motivated to seek self development, and see educational improvement as a stepping stone to better job opportunities. But this applies only to those who are confident enough to see that, for them, the job opportunities may be there.

The majority of adults, even in developed societies, are not necessarily so motivated. Even in terms of pure economism, in a context where wealth creation is concentrated in the hands of a shrinking and ever more skilled labour force, there should be concern to draw on the best talents available in whichever parts of society they may arise. If social justice or worries about social fragmentation are taken into account, then efforts should be greatly extended to increase motivation amongst excluded or marginalised groups. If Jackson's argument is accepted, then one way of doing this is through various kinds of civic education which reflect essentially local concerns. If an *adult learning* perspective is made the starting point, rather than training or education as separate and perhaps separated concepts, then the starting points must be the needs which the mainly local issues determine.

The essential educational components are those outlined in the previous chapter. Part of this is the list of skills for decision making which lead to openness, flexibility and personal confidence. This includes the confidence to go on to formal education as well as the confidence needed to play a full part in civic institutions: the one reinforces the other.

Using the framework outlined in chapter one, the rest of this chapter looks at the potential for developing and sustaining open learning in a variety of contexts. Is there a need, and if so in what places and in what ways, for educational programmes for adults which offer a training both for responsible citizenship and for individual growth and advancement? Where would the dual approach be both feasible and justifiable and what methods might be appropriate?

Developing and sustaining open learning

It was suggested above that the starting points for open learning must be the needs which local issues determine, and that these should be allied to the almost universal concern which exists for access to higher education, especially for currently excluded or marginalised groups. The argument put forward is that locally perceived needs, possibly by individuals and groups unmotivated towards education *per se*, must be built on in the interests both of building an inclusive citizenship and of maximising educational opportunities for individuals with underdeveloped talents. While generalisation about a multiplicity of local issues is not possible, some principles of procedure may be useful.

'Real' needs

First, there are very few places today where a programme designed for 1960s style 'nation building' would be appropriate. Even where societies like those of eastern Europe are in the process of rapid transformation and there is a strong desire to rebuild civil society, there may be resistance to the idea of adult education as an instrument for this direct purpose because of past experience of officially promoted propaganda. In these cases, education for democracy or the promotion of good government may be rejected unless it stems from local popular movements. In Africa in 1997, perhaps only in South Africa were there all the ingredients where there could be a successful repeat exercise like that of Kikuyu. In that country it might even be possible to use some of the Capricorn ideas (without the paternalism) in the interests of an inclusive citizenship which the Mandela-led Government wants to be multi-racial.

Secondly, popular movements for change where an element of planned adult learning can help, like those wishing to protect the environment or promote a more just gender balance, or better health through clean water; may be both global and local. Or they may be local, as where campaigns for minority and other human rights are directed at particular political regimes. If there is to be motivation to learn by those whose confidence is lacking, in most cases the impetus is more likely to come from active non-governmental organisations rather than the state itself. 'Real needs' are more likely to be discovered by working with existing NGOs than by starting from government agencies or from international organisations (however well meaning). The former students from Kikuyu were quite clear that any new initiatives in east Africa would have to be started by people like themselves: concerned citizens with a vision. And for them this vision extends to a reform of the present university systems where their children seem to be offered less than they had.

Providing agencies

Although this book has been written around a government-supported case study promoted by a University, it seems unlikely that this will be the normal approach for most countries into the next century. In the case of the UK, it is gratifying to be able to record that at least one University (Southampton) was in 1997 preparing to establish a 'New College' designed to facilitate access and develop individual confidence and motivation amongst a broad range of non-traditional students in the local community. And that these students will be 'the mainstream, majority student body'. The College will be 'student centred in its culture and planning' and provide a full programme of adult learning opportunities on an open entry basis. As currently planned, this could certainly be one way of promoting a new model of liberal adult education, appropriate both to its time and to its local context.[2]

Where similar university initiatives exist, this may be an appropriate way to proceed; but where universities take the view that they do not 'need' mature students or where there is little sense that they have a civic responsibility to appeal to wider communities or to the excluded, then alternative providers may have to be found. It may be a difficult task and new structures may have to be created. All that can be suggested here is the importance of contact with existing regional or international networks of adult education. At the time of writing, there were active regional organisations in almost all continents and there was a renewed and active interest in UNESCO in promoting adult learning opportunities of all kinds. There may also be an active local NGO network which will be able to facilitate access to others.*

Toleration by the controlling authorities

With the history of Kikuyu in mind, the authors felt this to be one of the most problematic of the ten conditions for sustainability. Certainly many initiatives which seek to build or re-build civil society may present challenges to the political status quo which the state authorities find unacceptable; that is a question of local political judgement. One useful concept in these circumstances is that of elbow room. The question to be asked is what can be done – what elbow room do we have- in any given context? For example, it may be possible to debate the uneven distribution of economic infrastructure or of water supplies as long as the first point of departure is not an attack on particular politicians. The one may be an acceptable part of the curriculum while the second may be condemned as subversion or incitement. The distinction between civic education and propaganda is sometimes difficult to maintain.

Financial support

Withdrawal of financial support was the final straw which broke the Kikuyu programme, not an outright ban. And it was of course also accompanied by political pressure and by disunity amongst the staff. Had there been a diversity of funding sources, as in the early days of the College, then it might have been possible to maintain or develop the programme rather than to close it. But the total reliance on government funds meant that government also effectively controlled policy. Those with a different mission or who wished to maintain the former mission could only have promoted their agendas if different sources of funds could have been found.

The lesson is clear. A combined public/private initiative is likely to have more freedom of action than one dependent on government alone. In fact it is a diversity of funding sources which offers the greatest strength in the face of a hostile or indifferent polity.

Staff understanding of the mission

It has been shown that at Kikuyu the mission was assumed rather than taught or even made explicit. There was no staff training or induction which might have stimulated debate or constructive change. Instead, when new staff were recruited who had a more technicist approach, who saw 'adult education' as a set of skills which could be taught to anybody who wanted to be a professional adult educator, the argument for civic education was lost before the debate could begin.** It

*E.g. The Asia/South Pacific Bureau for Adult Education, or the Consejo de Education de Adultos de America Latina. An example of a local organisation is the Development Network of Indigenous Voluntary Associations (DENIVA) in Uganda.

**The approach of 'andragogy', then favoured in the USA. See Knowles 1968, 1980

was easier to opt for a generic training and to avoid the difficult and probably contentious issue of why,what and how, particular adults wish to learn.

Nevertheless, the right kind of staff development and training is the *sine qua non* of any future successful programmes of civic education of the kind we have described. The early staff at Kikuyu had absorbed a particular mission, curriculum and approach through their similar previous professional and cultural experiences. However, in the absence of any effective staff induction or training their was an eventual breakdown in common understanding of the mission.

In a discussion amongst the authors, Patrick Muzaale made an interesting comment about the staff of whom he had experience as a student in 1965–66, that they seemed so *committed* to the task of teaching; this raised the related question about how you teach a sense of values – which underpinned the commitment – in their absence. As Patrick Muzaale put it, 'the tendency has been to focus on technical abilities; but values are neglected. We train very brilliant accountants who know how to steal everything within reach. The technology for teaching this other capacity appears to be elusive . . .'

One answer seems to be that the teaching staff must be aware of the purposes which motivate the learners, how these mesh with their own values, and how best to construct educational programmes which are then learner-centred. Houle's analysis of 'misapplied systems'[3] is a useful reminder of some of the things which adult education is not: including public relations or a vaguely defined idea of 'service'. No adult education system can survive if the system itself is seen as its main reason for existence: and yet that can happen if the training which supports it is not rooted in the local contextual realities. Staff must at least empathise with and frequently share the purposes which motivate the learners in their local context. This may happen in part because learners and staff share the same values. If they do not, there has to be some attempt to introduce the worthwhileness of these purposes and values as part of the training. There can be no effective programmes or training which are out of context or where the purposes of learning are ignored.

In conducting a recent study of *Training Adult Educators in African Universities*[4] it became clear that the most effective training was done where there was either a clear policy framework in place for the development of adult education, or where the programmes for which the training had been offered had been determined. Where training was both generic and out of context it was not clear either to the training institutions or to the trainees what purposes the training was meant to serve.

Learner participation

At Kikuyu, learner participation was assured, because of the access provided to higher education and to self improvement. Within the programme there had to be some confidence building, even for these already ambitious students. But participation by such students is not difficult to ensure in any society. What has to be worked at is participation by those who lack confidence or who do not see opportunities within the programmes on offer as 'access' courses. For example, an unemployed person may, above all, want a job. But until there is a readiness to learn the necessary skills, the individual may not see adult learning as relevant. It is here that Jackson's point quoted above comes into play. Students motivated to learn because of their activity as citizens can and do move on to wanting an access course for themselves. This phenomenon was observed in work undertaken by Wayne State University in Detroit in the1970s with automobile workers. Similar programmes were later taken up by the Ford Motor Company in both Britain and America where workers were offered any kind of education of their choice, partly because of the readiness this induced in individual workers for other kinds of training and education.[5]* A liberal curriculum does open windows for the learners in a way which enhances their perception of what is possible.

A relevant curriculum

The key principle of procedure is negotiation between all the stakeholders. The authors do not pretend that this applied at all stages at Kikuyu, and in that sense any success achieved was a lucky accident. But there were always the allied principles of flexibility and student centredness which did operate, and which did change the curriculum at crucial moments: for example, the early recognition of vocational motivation and the importance of enhancing communication skills, especially in the English language. If instead of a pre-determined curriculum thought to be 'liberal', programme planners start from learner interests, then the possible starting points are as varied as the whole range of human curiosity and wanting to know. The questions to be asked are: what are these potential learners doing or what do they want to see happen; how can planned adult learning help and be seen to help; will that increase confidence, decision making skills and the ability to change both themselves and their environment?

An adequate range of learning materials?

Open learning systems are no longer confined to library access or face to face teaching, important though these continue to be. However, in some countries, certainly in sub-Saharan Africa, and elsewhere in countries devastated by war or economic collapse, libraries at all levels have broken down to the point where it will take years to replenish stocks lost or not kept up to date. And this shortage of materials can induce a feeling of helplessness. This means that different media assume an even greater importance in such countries than they do in more fortunate or richer places. And not only computers or the Internet, but also the older and cheaper television and radio. In all cases planners have to start with what is available and what is affordable. And in all cases there is always the resource of the learners themselves. The principle of procedure here is to match up local knowledge and intuitive understanding with what can be made available by others; not forgetting international organisations like the Commonwealth of

*In 1996 ther were more than 700 similar Employee Development Schemes in the UK alone

Learning which offers Commonwealth countries the use of distance teaching packages across national boundaries.

Rethinking the learning environment

The learning environment at Kikuyu was thought to be ideal because of the collegiate atmosphere, a building which was open and welcoming and with easy access to a good library. In other words it was residential adult education at its best, where all the members of the College learned from each other as well as from the offered curriculum. But already in 1961 there was use of other media, especially radio, without which there would have been less discussion about the issues of the day in the informal atmosphere of coffee breaks on the grass shared by both staff and students. It has to be asked what was learned from the fact of residence and what could be done in other ways.

There is no substitute for periods of intensive study in a residential setting; this was a key factor in making Kikuyu a turning point in the lives of so many learners. Not only is it possible for all participants to learn from each other and to stimulate each other in challenging cherished assumptions or the use of evidence in debate. It is also possible to do this at the level of mutual respect and social equality. But Open Universities have shown that much can be done in other ways like correspondence courses, the use of pre-packaged information via these, or cassettes or radio or television. And the increased availability of computers and the Internet will open up even more possibilities in the future. Residence remains a vital component and, for the few, it may remain the best way to study at almost any level. But residence is not only expensive, it also disrupts the lives of those who take part which, in maturity, may outweigh the advantages of residential study. Short periods of residence, including face to face tuition, combined with the systematic use of other media seems to be the sensible – and affordable – way forward in most cases.

Thus new and sustainable structures do not need to include new buildings, rather the imaginative use of existing ones; teaching can and should be interactive and include some face to face tuition without the creation of new premises. Open Universities have shown that residence does not have to be over a long period to be effective. Multi-media approaches are important for themselves in giving access to information technology, but also because they are likely to be more efficient as part of a total delivery system with much shorter periods of residence than one academic year. The Kikuyu short courses of only three weeks did have a transformative effect in some individual cases and showed what could be done in a very short period by way of opening windows and increasing readiness to learn.

Because the civic part of all this is unlikely to be inspired by government (except in rare cases like South Africa where the new nation-state is important), then the greatest commitment is likely to come from NGOs backed by the private sector.

Futures?

The conditions for sustainability are dynamic and shifting. Over time, the real needs of stakeholders, the mission of providing agencies, the degree of permissiveness of the controlling authorities, the amount of financial support available, the competence and attitudes of the available teaching staff and the attractiveness of programmes are bound to change.

In the case of east Africa, current circumstances suggest that if a Kikuyu – type programme were to be recreated, it would have to be organised as a private effort independent of government and University. The case for openness and flexibility in civic education is unlikely to be made by modern universities per se, who are more interested in coping with the flow of young undergraduates or in maintaining their research budgets. In this regard, the former students and beneficiaries of this particular programme wanted to play an active part in organising such an effort when this was discussed with then in 1995; their contribution to be particularly in the areas of advocacy, resource mobilisation and project promotion. They argued that the continuing need to equip people for a continuously changing technological environment and for a role in civil society alike, calls for such an initiative.

Notes

[1]In Walters S (Ed) 1997 : 54
[2]University of Southampton 1997
[3]Houle 1972 : 25–26
[4]Fordham 1997
[5]Fordham *et al* 1976

Appendix 1

Extract from Memorandum of Association of the College of Citizenship Corporation of Kenya

The objects for which the Company is established are:

(a) the principal objects aforesaid are (and are hereinafter referred to as "the Principal Objects") to found establish and carry on in the Colony and Protectorate of Kenya colleges or institutions unconnected with any political party or any particular religious sectarian or racial creed doctrine or opinion for the education of adults of all races and creeds in economics, political and social theory and history and for promoting the study and general knowledge among the students of such colleges or institutions of subjects relating to the progress and development of communities and of mankind generally including without prejudice to the generality of the forgoing political economic and social science, statistics, history, jurisprudence, agriculture, biology, ecology, health, urbanisation, local and central government and any other subjects whether academic, vocational or partly academic and partly vocational which will assist students to become useful intelligent and active members of society with qualities of leadership and a sense of common citizenship among members of different races through better understanding free from any bias of the common economic, social, administrative and social problems of their country.

(b) the objects of the Company ancillary to the Principal Objects are such of the following as are charitable by the law of England and the law of Kenya to provide for the delivery and holding of lectures, exhibitions, public meetings, classes, study circles, conferences and courses to further the Principal Objects to grant scholarships and bursaries and to provide residential accommodation for students of such colleges or institutions.

(28 July 1960)

Appendix 2

Policy Statement for the Institute of Adult Studies July 1967

1. The University College and Adult Education

The involvement of University College in Adult Education is one part of its total commitment to national development. Not only must it train and educate the nation's high level manpower and act as a centre of research: it must also extend the influence of the University to the Community as a whole. There are many reasons why this should be so. Among the most important are:-

a) Helping to bridge the gap between the highly educated minority and the majority of the people. The College must serve the needs of the whole nation, not just the few who are fortunate enough to become full time students or teachers there.

b) Enrichment of University teachers themselves, by establishing close contacts with the society they serve. This may well be important in the development of new concepts, syllabuses and inter-disciplinary studies for undergraduate teaching.

c) Helping to create an *informed* public opinion without which there can be no effective popular participation in government.

2. Priorities for the Institute of Adult Studies

The educational needs of adults are many and varied. With its limited resources the Institute cannot hope to meet them all: indeed it would be folly for it to try to do so. In particular, we do not intend to act as a substitute secondary school, a task which others can do better and at less cost. We intend to do those things, and only those things which can be done better by a university than by any other institution. The main tasks we have set ourselves for the next triennium are as follows:-

a) **Remedial education** at the highest level for those whose educational opportunities have been inadequate. This will be done through extra-mural classes, residential courses and correspondence/radio instruction. Those seeking general educational qualifications will work towards the *Certificate of Adult Studies* and some will proceed either to university entrance or to part-time undergraduate studies: others may be helped towards success in professional examinations, while others may be encouraged to continue with their general education without necessarily having an examination oriented goal.

b) **Continuing Education** for those whose formal education is completed or who have reached positions of responsibility. Such courses or seminars will be aimed particularly at those who make decisions in our society, whether they be in government, politics, industry or voluntary organisations. A university must be both independent and concerned in this. It has a unique opportunity to bring together leaders from different departments and organisations on neutral ground to discuss, for example, development problems.

c) Acting as a **service agency** for other organisations engaged in adult education. Extra Mural tutors stationed in their areas are in an advantageous position to advise on adult education problems and to bring to the attention of District Training Centres, for example, information about the latest methods and ideas in the teaching of adults.

Acting as a service agency may also involve the direct provision of courses where local skills are not yet developed. One of the main functions of the *Correspondence Course Unit* will be to establish new standards of excellence and professional skills in a previous neglected field.

d) **Professional Training and Research** will also be developed during the triennium 1967–70. The Institute of Adult Studies must become a centre for the study of adult education in all its aspects. Training should involve both the participation of the Institute in the teacher training of the Department of Education and the provision of common foundation courses for all extension workers.

Research *must* include investigation into needs and priorities as indicated by the Government's Board of Adult Education.

Appendix 3

A course-by-course analysis of students' schooling, qualifications and careers

Key to Abbreviations

BoG	Board of Governors
CDO	Community Development Officer
Cor	Correspondence
CPK	Church of the Province of Kenya
Ctr	Controller
Dip Lib	Diploma in Librarianship
Dip Soc Wk	Diploma in Social Work
Dist. Serv. Comm.	District Service Commission
DO	District Officer
DSM	Dar es Salaam
EMS	Extra-mural studies
JS	Junior secondary
KBS	Kenya Broadcasting Service
KIA	Kenya Institute of Administration
KNLS	Kenya National Library Service
Mak	Makerere
Nbi	Nairobi
PCEA	Presbyterian Church of East Africa
Prim TT	Primary teacher training
Princ. Doc. Off.	Principal Documentation Officer
Reg.	Regional
TTC	Teacher Training College
VOK	Voice of Kenya

A course-by-course analysis of students' schooling, qualifications and careers

1962/63

NAME	AGE	SCHOOLING	JOB	P. STUDY	QUAL	JOB 1	JOB 2	LAST JOB	VOL WORK
Buzabalyawo (U)	26	O level	Housing Manager	HSC (Cor)	BA (Econ)	Junior Manager	Accountant	Airline Finance Ctr.	
Gwayambadde (U)	39	Primary TT	Primary Teacher		B.Litt (Oxon)	Univ. Lecturer	Anglican Priest	Died	Clan Leader
Kabuye (U)	33	Primary 3	Housing Manager	O Level	BA (Econ)	Econ. Analyst (Esso)	Coop Manager	Univ. Hall Warden	
Kibuka, Katie (U)	40	Primary	President YWCA		Failed Dip SW	Ran Women's Coop		Died	
Mwakina	33	Primary	Clerk		Com Course	Clerk			
Okach	25	Primary	Clerk		MA (Edin)	University Lecturer		Died	Union Officer
Opundo	24	Secondary	Asst. Court Reg.			Army Officer Cadet			

1963/64

NAME	AGE	SCHOOLING	JOB	P STUDY	QUAL	JOB 1	JOB 2	LAST JOB	VOL WORK
Buluda (T)	2?		Teacher		MA (USA)			Hist. Lect. UDSM	
Isiaho	29	JS2	Asst. Chief	EMS	Ind Rel (Ruskin)	Teacher	FTC Principal	County Councillor	11 entries
Kedikilwe (B)		Secondary			BA (Conn)	Civil Service	Director Personnel	Minister, Pres.Off.	
Latim (U)								Died	
Mutengu (U)	2?	Prim TT	Teacher		TT (Leics)/ MEd (Mak)	Teacher	Sec. Head	Reg. Prime Minister	
Oluoch	27	Primary	Asst. Stationmaster	Accounts	BA (Mak)/Dip Lib (Aber)	Librarian		Director, KNLS	Chair. BoG Sec Sch
Osundwa	29	Prim TT	P1		BA (Nbi)	Lecturer KIA	Prin. Doc. Off, KBS	Farmer	BoG/CPK Synod
Ouma, N	2?	Prim TT	Teacher		BA Ed (Mak)	Sec Teacher	Dep. Principal TTC	Died (1993)	

1964/65

NAME	AGE	SCHOOLING	JOB	P STUDY	QUAL	JOB 1	JOB 2	LAST JOB	VOL WORK
Kabetu, Rose					Dip Lib (Aber)				
Kabole									
Kayila									
Kibaki		Seminary	Trainee Priest		Dip Lib (Aber)	Librarian		Died	
Njeha		Secondary	PO Clerk		BA (Nbi)	Post Office			
Sanya									

1965/66

NAME	AGE	SCHOOLING	JOB	P STUDY	QUAL	JOB 1	JOB 2	LAST JOB	VOL WORK
Agik	40	Dip Fine Art			BA (Nbi)	CDO ?		Died	
Macharia	25				Dip Soc Wk (Mak)	CDO		Retired 94	
Muzaale (U)	26	Jun Sec	Railway Guard	EMS	PhD (Calif)	Bank Trainee	Lecturer	Professor (Mak)	Chair: 3 national com.
Naigere (U)	27	Prim TT	Headmaster		BA (Econ) Mak	Bank Trainee	CDO	Church Coop Off.	Chair: Cathedral Congregation
Okoko	25				CAS				
Okoth	40				Dip Soc Wk (Mak)				
Otieno	27				Dip Soc Wk (Mak)	DO			
Raphoto (SA)	24	Primary			PhD (Syrac)	Univ. Grad. Ass.	Priv. Consultant	Dep. Dir. Literacy Prop.	Quaker overseas service

1966/67

NAME	AGE	SCHOOLING	JOB	P STUDY	QUAL	JOB 1	JOB 2	LAST JOB	VOL WORK
Ayoo	26	Prim TT	P3 teacher	O Level Cor/EMS	BA& Dip Ed (Nbi)	Sec. Teacher	Dep Head	Head	
Gathaiya					Failed CAS				
Gor			TU Officer		Ruskin ?		MP		
Kiagayu						Ed, Coast Standard	Died		
Kigge (U)	31	Jun Sec	Asst. Stationmaster		BA (Mak)	Admin. Civil Servant	Sec. to Cabinet	Lnd Rst Tsk Fce, Plce Ten Bd *	
Kinyua								KCC retired	
Ming'ala									
Mugweru	32	Prim TT	Clerk	HSC Cor	Dip Soc Wk (Mak)	Lab Officer	CC Admin.	Univ. Admin	
Mutulu									
Mwandoro									
Mwath	32	Prim TT (T2)	Clerk, City Council	Dip Soc Wk (Mak)	Teacher	Kenyatta UC Admin.	Retired		
Ngaywa (U)				BA			EM Resident Tutor	Died	
Ochieng									
Ogore									
Okoth (U)	29	Prim TT	Teacher	Cor	MA (Hull)	Univ EM Organiser	Bank Trainer	Chair Dist Serv Com	
Ruben						VOK ?			
1 failed CAS									

* Chair of Land Resettlement Task Force and Police Tender Board

1967/68

NAME	AGE	SCHOOLING	JOB	P STUDY	QUAL	JOB 1	JOB 2	LAST JOB	VOL WORK
Ambole	25	O level	Rail Inspector	C&G Civ Eng	BA (Nbi)	Youth Off	Var Admin/Tng.	Dep. Com. Social Serv.	Various socie-ties
Gaitho									
Karanja	24	O level	Lib Ass		B Com (Nbi)	Var. Indust	Marketing Advisor	Marketing Manager	
Kihenja						DO ?			
Kiragu		Primary	Primary Head		Failed CAS				Mau Mau Freedom Fighter
Malula (T)					B Com (Dar) ?				
Matsanza						NCCK		Died 94, USA	
Mayombwe (T)									
M'Marete	32	Prim TT	Dr Barn/P2		CAS/Coop Tng	VOK Prod Ass	Editor Farm Coop		BoG TTC
Mmbulika		Prim TT	Teacher	BA Ed (Nbi)	Teacher	TTC Tutor		Died	
Muguiyi	30	Prim TT	P1	Cor/EMS	B Ed (Mak)	Sec. Teacher	Head	TTC Lecturer	BoG Tech. Inst/Sec. Sch.
Mungai	22	Sec School	Univ Clerk		LLB (Nbi)	Asst. Reg. Nbi. Univ.	Chief Admin, Moi	Advocate	
Mwangi					BA Ed (Mak)		TTC Tutor	Died	
Njoroge	23	O Level		Clerk	BA (Mak)	DO	Var. Admin.	Dep Sec Home Affairs	

1967/68 continued

NAME	AGE	SCHOOLING	JOB	P STUDY	QUAL	JOB 1	JOB 2	LAST JOB	VOL WORK
Nzusyo						Post Office	Child Welfare	Died	
Okumbe							Econ. Tax Dept	Died	
Omuse						MoA			
Ong'injo-D'Aw		O Level	Clerk		B Com, Nairobi/MBA in USA	Civil service	Under Sec. Min. of Finance	Permanent Sec. of Culture & S.S.	
Reche	24	Sec TT	Teacher		Ed D (Virg Poly)	Head	Res. Tut. Univ. Nbi.	Univ. lect. Ed Admin	BoG TTC
Sande-Jowi	26	O Level	Loans Officer	A Level (cor)	B Ed (Mak)	Teacher	Head	Asst. Dir.	Patron of various groups
Wanjala					LLB (Nbi)			Lawyer	
4 failed CAS									

1968

NAME	AGE	SCHOOLING	JOB	P STUDY	QUAL	JOB 1	JOB 2	LAST JOB	VOL WORK
Amunga	25	Prim TT	Teacher	A Level	MA (Nbi)	Head	Planning Officer	Planning Director	Coop Secretary
Ayoki	34	Prim TT	P1	O Level	S1	TTC Tutor	Head	Head (Retd.)	Land Elder, Coop/Church Com
Buleemi		Primary	Teacher	O Level	LLB	Law Tutor	Town Clerk	Lorry Driver	
Dhliwayo (Z)					PhD (A.Bel)				
Gakure									
Gitaka									
Ita		Prim TT	Chief	O Level	BA Ed (Nbi)	Ind. Management	Head IPC	Head EPZ	Nairobi Council, BoG,
Kapere	26	Prim TT	P2	O Level	MSc (Man)	Teacher	Admin.	Univ. Dep. Registrar	
Kariuki							NYS Commandant	Shell Accounts ?	
Kibutu							TTC Tutor	Head	
Kilavuka	26	Prim TT	P1		BA Ed (Nbi)	Teacher	Teacher	Teacher	
Mbai-Rucha		Secondary	Teacher	TT	CAS/Dip Man	Manager	General Manager	Gen. Man. (S Sellers)	
Mugweru	27	O Level	Sales	HSC	CAS	Book Editor	Book Editor	Bookshop Owner	
Musembi								KANU HQ ?	
Musiga							Welfare Dept, Nakuru	Died	
Mutweke						Teacher ?			
Mwangi					BA Ed (Mak)	TTC Tutor	Died		
Mwaniki	30	Prim TT	Head	O&A Cor	BA Ed (Nbi)	EM Org.	CDO	Ass. Univ. Registrar	

1968 continued

NAME	AGE	SCHOOLING	JOB	P STUDY	QUAL	JOB 1	JOB 2	LAST JOB	VOL WORK
Nyaoke	30	Jun Sec	Stationmaster	EMS	MA (Nbi)	Rail Supervisor	Soc. Service Director	Dep Town Clerk	YMCA/ Kisumu Link Committee
Olewe	26	O Level	Bank Clerk		CAS	Teacher	Head	Died	Chairman KNUT, Kisumu D
Omolo	25?	Prim TT	Teacher		B Ed (Nbi)	Teacher	TTC Tutor		
Otieno	30?					VOK Ac. Ed.		Farmer ?	
Ouma B	30?		KAR			Sec. Teacher		Died	
Owako ("Molly")	29	O Level	Ass Librarian		Dip Lib (Mak)	Librarian	Librarian	Head, MacMillan	
Ruta (T)	30?			LLB (Dar)	Lawyer ? ?				
Saropa						Librarian Met HQ	–		
Sikinyi	25	O Level	Clerk	Acc Cor	CAS	Accounts	Loans Officer	Finance Manager	
Simiyu			Teacher					Retired	
2 failed CAS									

1969

NAME	AGE	SCHOOLING	JOB	P STUDY	QUAL	JOB 1	JOB 2	LAST JOB	VOL WORK
Abonyo	31	Prim TT	Teacher		BA,Dip Ed (Nbi)	Teacher	SEO MoE	Priv .Business	BoG, Dep. Returning Off.
Ajwang-Odong	28	Secondary	Cashier		BA Ed (Nbi)	Bank Manager	Bank Manager	Sec.KBA	Various Welfare Soc
Bodo	25	O Level/TT	P1		Dip Ed (Kenyatta)	Teacher	Dep. Head	Head	
Chebri			Clerk		Post Office ?				
Gachunga	33	Jun Sec	Health Ass	O Level Cor	Dip, Solid Waste	Trade Officer	Cleansing Sup.	Solid Waste	Manager
Gichuru	33	Agric Cert	Ag Ass	Cor	BA (Nbi)	DO	Asst. Secretary	Under Secretary	
Kaburu									
Kadionyi	25	Prim TT	Teacher		CAS	Teacher	Teacher	Retired	Church Leader
Karani									
Kazungu						Teacher			
Kibui					BA Ed (Nbi)	Sec Teacher			
Kinyanjui J		S1	Teacher	BA Ed (Nbi)	Harbours DSM	University Admin	Dep. Registrar		DSM Admin
Kirunja									
Machira					LLB (DSM)			Advocate	
Maina					BA Ed (Nbi)	Teacher			

1969 continued

NAME	AGE	SCHOOLING	JOB	P STUDY	QUAL	JOB 1	JOB 2	LAST JOB	VOL WORK
Mibei	35	O Level/TT	Teacher	O Level	LLB	Magistrate	MP	Adv. Complaints Com.	
Muchiri							Dean TTC	Dean PCEA TTC	
Mwingisi	29	Prim TT	Teacher	O Level Cor	BA Ed (Nbi),Dip(Edin)	TTC Tutor	Dep Principal	Principal	
Mwiti									
Nderitu									
Ndung'u	40?		Police ?						
Njeru J									
Njeru R									
Odhiambo	25		Clerk		CAS	Journalist AFP	Journalist AFP	Journalist AFP	
Oloo		Primary	Teacher	O Level Cor	BA,Dip Ed (Nbi)			Dep. Director, Ministry of Education	
Owiti	30?		TU Off		LLB (Nbi)		Director Ind Rel	Died	
1 failed CAS									

A note on methodology

1 **Tracing former students**

The starting points were the Annual Reports of the College, which all contained pass lists and admission figures for the long course. A gap exists for 1964–65 for which no Annual Report was available. Names for this year group were compiled from the memories of Godfrey Muriuki and Paul Fordham as was information about the career paths of former students. Without the set of Annual Reports, tracing would have been a formidable task. Of the total of approximately 130 students, the 10 students for whom no names are available are presumed to have failed both the mature age entrance and the CAS examinations. Including these 10, there is no information on 26 of the 130 former students. The possible total from whom career path information might be obtained was therefore104.

The March 1995 'Re-union and Seminar' was advertised in the Kenyan press and in Uganda amongst known former students (the great majority of former students were from Kenya). Additionally, John Fox placed an article in the Sunday Nation on: *One of a Kind: Remembering a very special kind of college*, and also published an interview with former student Silas Ita. The various press items attracted a good response from those within easy travelling distance from Nairobi and more than twenty students attended the seminar.

2 **Bio-data and interviews of former students**

Bio-data forms and interview schedules were used to ensure consistency of data for the numbers of students recorded above. There is full information on 54 students (one of whom has died since being interviewed). There is partial information on 50, (of who 17 are known to have died). Of the 54, a total of 30 has been interviewed.

All interviews were tape recorded with 21 individual or group interviews taking place at the Seminar. To produce a better regional balance, later interviews were conducted by Tom Mulusa in western Kenya during 1995–96. All the student interviews were undertaken by people who had been members of staff at Kikuyu (Fordham, Fox and Mulusa) An attempt was made to have the four Tanzanian students interviewed, but this proved abortive,. One very late (and partial) interview took place at a chance meeting in Hamburg in the plenary session of the UNESCO Adult Education Conference in 1997; this is included in the total of 30.

3 **Interviews of former staff**

Except for that of Tom Mulusa, all of these were conducted by Patrick Muzaale, either in Nairobi or in/from the UK. An agreed interview schedule was used and three of the interviews were by long distance telephone (to Brussels, Copenhagen and London). All the interviews were tape recorded. Interestingly, the telephoned interviews were crisper and yielded just as much information as those done face to face. There was thus considerable cost saving without any sacrifice of data quality.

4 **Writing Strategy** was agreed at two three-day workshops (in Kampala and Nairobi) in 1996 and 1997.

Bibliography

Bertelsen P, Fordham P, and London J, 1977, *Evaluation of the Wayne State University's University Studies and Weekend College Programme,* UNESCO, Paris

Blumler J, 1962, *The Effects of Long-Term Residential Adult Education in Post-War Britain,* Unpublished PhD thesis, University of Oxford

Colonial Office,1945, *Higher Education in West Africa* (the Elliott Report), Cmd. 6655, HMSO, London

Colonial Office,1948, *Education for Citizenship in Africa,* Co. No. 216, HMSO, London

Darkenwald G, and Merriam S, 1982, *Adult Education: Foundations of Practice,* Harper, New York

Delors J (Chair), 1996, *Learning: The Treasure Within,* UNESCO Publishing, Paris

Faure E (Chair), 1972, *Learning to Be,* Unesco, Paris

Field J, (ed.),1991, *Learning Citizenship,* Department of Continuing Education, University of Warwick

Fordham P, Fox J, and Muzaale P, 1995, *Report of a Reunion and Seminar,* INCED, University of Warwick, Coventry

Fieldhouse R, 1985, *Adult Education and the Cold War*, University of Leeds

Fordham P, 1964, 'The English Tradition' in *Adult Education*, XXXVII, 2

Gertzel C, 1970, *The Politics of Independent Kenya,* EAPH, Nairobi and Heinemann, London

Hall S and Held D, 1989, *Citizens and Citizenship* in Hall S and Jacques M (Ed.) *New Times,* Lawrence and Wishart, London

Hooper J, Farrell J, Hedge A, and Thorpe T, 1995, *Can They Do That? Learning About Active Citizenship,* Citizenship Foundation and NIACE, Leicester

Houle C, 1972, *The Design of Education*, Jossey-Bass, San Francisco

Hunter G, 1967, *The Best of Both Worlds,* OUP for the Institute of Race Relations, London

Hunter G, 1969, *Modernising Peasant Societies,* OUP for the Institute of Race Relations, London

Kibaki, Mwai, in a lecture on *Education and National Development* to 'The Kenya We Want Convention' August 1962

Mphahlele E, 1963, 'Travels of an Extra-Mural Donkey', *Transition,* November, Kampala

Ranson S, 1994, *Towards the Learning Society,* Cassell, London

Schools Council 1968 *Enquiry 1, Young School Leavers,* HMSO, London

Stirling D, 1957 *Proposals for the Future* Capricorn Africa Society, Nairobi

Stromquist N, 1997, *Literacy for Citizenship,* State University of New York

Titmus C, and Steele T, 1995, *Adult Education for Independence,* Leeds Studies in Continuing Education, University of Leeds

University of Southampton, 1997, Paper on 'The Establishment of New College'

Usher R, Bryant I, and Johnston R,1997, *Adult Education and the Postmodern Challenge,* Routledge, London

Walters S (ed.), 1997, *Globalization, Adult Education and Training,* NIACE, Leicester

Wangoola P 1980, *The College of Social Studies: The Political Economy of a Residential College of Adult Education in Kenya,* Unpublished paper prepared as a graduate student in the University of Southampton

Wiltshire H, 1961, *Centre to Aid People of Colony,* report in East African Standard, 21 June

Wiltshire H, 1961b, College Development Plan (mimeo)

Wiltshire H, 1962, Paper on the CSS and the projected Extra-Mural Department, 24 April (mimeo)

Wiltshire H, 1963, 'Adult Education in Kenya: A Fresh Start', reprinted in Rogers A, 1976, *The Spirit and the Form,* University of Nottingham, Department of Adult Education

Wiltshire H, Taylor J, and Jennings B, 1980, *The 1919 Report,* University of Nottingham, Department of Adult Education

Index

About the authors

Paul Fordham is Honorary Professor at the University of Warwick. After ten years in adult education at the University of Nottingham, he worked in universities in Uganda and Kenya before eighteen years as Director of Adult Education at the University of Southampton. He has been a consultant in many different countries, especially in Africa and Asia. He is an Honorary Life Member and former Chair of the Executive of NIACE.

John Fox is the Director of Intermedia Ltd in Nairobi, a training and consultancy organisation he established in 1988. He started in university adult education at Nottingham in the 1960s, from where he was seconded for two years (1967–69) as Tutor at the College of Social Studies, Kikuyu. Until his return to Kenya, he was from 1973 at the University of Southampton, where he established an adult education training and research unit. His various international consultancies have taken him to Botswana, Ghana, India, Nepal, Papua New Guinea, Uganda, Sierra Leone and Tanzania.

Patrick Muzaale now chairs the Uganda Public Service Commission but at the time of writing this book was Professor of Social Work and Social Administration at Makerere University. He did not complete secondary school and was working as a railway guard when he enrolled at the College of Social Studies in 1965. After a first degree in Uganda he studied at the University of Manchester and gained his PhD at Berkeley in California. He worked for a time as consultant for the Commonwealth Secretariat in Trinidad, helping to establish a new university department; but most of his academic career has been in Uganda.

A Bad Hand Played Well

How To Own Your 90,000 Hours At Work

Advance Reviews

"A kind and thoughtful people-focused antidote to the $1Tn global problem of burnout at work, offering insights for a life well-lived instead."

KoAnn Vikoren Skrzyniarz
Founder & Chief Executive Officer, Sustainable Brands

"I would recommend this book to anyone looking to maximise intentional living and minimise regret."

Kian Bakhtiari
Founder, The People

"Get ready to embark on a life-changing adventure with this extraordinary book. By embracing the power of actionable kindness, you'll navigate the ever-evolving landscape, redefine your sense of self, and truly make the most of every moment in your journey."

Quinn O'Brien
Chief Marketing Officer, Carnegie Learning